A World of Change

THE CROMWELL FAMILY
1485–1658

John Cooper and
Susan Morris

Education Department
National Portrait Gallery

Series editor: Rosemary Kelly

How to u...	
Cromwell or Crumbwell?	3
Thomas Cromwell or Thomas Smyth?	8
'Trusty and right well-beloved counsellor'	12
Traitors and gentlemen	20
The Cromwell family: 1540–1640	24
Ironsides	30
Lord-General and Lord Protector	34
'Let God be Judge between you and me!'	44
Find out more for yourself	50
Index	51

This book follows the family history of the Cromwells over about one hundred and fifty years. It discusses how they arranged their marriages, brought up their children and dealt with their relatives.

Like many other families, the Cromwells grew in wealth and importance during this time and, like others, they had some setbacks too. However, they were different from most other families in that they produced two men who each had an enormous influence on their country. Both were at the centre of government during their lifetimes: the first was Thomas Cromwell, a brewer's son who became Henry VIII's chief minister, and the second was his great great great nephew, Oliver Cromwell, who became Lord Protector of England, Scotland and Ireland. How did this affect their families? We shall see.

Stanley Thornes (Publishers) Ltd

How to use this book

Everybody has a family tree, but whether they know the details of it or not is a different matter. If you are curious about yours, you can begin to research it easily through birth, death and marriage certificates, photographs, gravestones, letters, parish registers and so on. Ideally you would also look at artefacts such as houses, clothes, furniture, as well as portraits or written documents, but the further back in time you go, the harder it becomes. This is particularly true of the Cromwell family for two reasons.

Firstly, the Cromwells covered in this book lived so long ago that many of their own records and possessions will have worn out, decayed or disappeared. Most of the London in which Thomas, and later, Oliver, spent so much time was destroyed during the Great Fire of 1666 and the bombing during the Second World War. Added to this, there was deliberate destruction of much of Thomas' and Oliver's property (including their corpses) after their deaths; neither of them has a tomb. Secondly, because they were politically so important, most of the people writing about them at the time were more interested in that side of their lives, rather than in their families. So the evidence included in this book is mostly documentary and has had to be collected from a great many sources – it cannot be found all together in one place.

In the sixteenth and seventeenth centuries, when Thomas and Oliver were alive, the lives of English people were affected by the level of society to which they belonged. Roughly, there were four 'sorts': nobles, townspeople and merchants, yeomen and peasants. Which 'sort' you belonged to would affect how your family felt and acted on such things as marriage, children, education, employment and inheritance. Thomas and Oliver are interesting because they 'moved up' the order. Therefore as you go through this book, look out for signs which show that their family ideas changed. As well as looking at family relationships, remember to look 'from the outside' to see what people who were not members of the family felt about them and their rise.

Is the evidence included here biased? We have tried to indicate in the text where we think it might be, for example when a hostile person's words are used. Other biases come from the gaps; a lot of information about the Cromwells has disappeared. With our twentieth-century minds we have tried to work out what sixteenth- and seventeenth-century people found important; we might have misunderstood. If, before you began reading this book, you already had a mental picture of what you thought Oliver Cromwell or Thomas Cromwell was like, then there is already the bias of a preformed idea in your head too!

The cover pictures are Thomas Cromwell *after Hans Holbein (National Portrait Gallery, London) and* Oliver Cromwell *by Samuel Cooper (Bridgeman Art Library/private collection).*

Cromwell or Crumbwell?

One way to begin studying a family is to look at the surname. It can offer information about them. As you probably know, some surnames give clues to the family trade or job, for example 'Brewer'. Before about 1400, ordinary people did not use fixed surnames as we do today. Instead you might be called 'Robert of York' or 'John the Butcher' to identify you; but other people in your family need not have York or Butcher as their surname if something else was better. In England around the time when Thomas Cromwell was born (c. 1485), the new habit of having a family surname passed by parents to children (as we do today) was becoming more usual but, as you will see, it was still not a fixed rule. However, the choice of 'Cromwell' as a surname is a clue to what identified this particular family: it is thought that the Cromwells took their name from the village of Cromwell in Nottinghamshire.

The next question is, does 'Cromwell' actually mean anything? Some places are named after a founder, village chief or local landowner: for example, 'Breaston' in Derbyshire comes from 'Braegd's Tun', or the village of Braegd – an Anglo-Saxon chief. So the name Cromwell might have commemorated an important person.

In fact, 'Cromwell' probably comes from where the village was, rather than who lived there. In Old English the word 'crumb' means crooked and 'wella' means stream – so 'Cromwell' is the 'village of the crooked stream'.

1 'Cromwell' as a surname would only have been useful once the person had left the village. Why?

2 In what ways might it be useful to have a fixed family surname as we do today? How would you change your surname today if you wanted to?

3 In 1538 Thomas Cromwell sent out orders that every baptism, marriage and burial had to be recorded in the parish register. Who would keep this register? Would these registers be useful for finding out your own family tree?

4 Following the 1836 Act for the Registration of Births, Deaths and Marriages, the government began to build up a full record of all its citizens for the first time. Where are these records kept? Where do parents go to register the birth of a baby and its full name? Within how many days after birth must they do this?

How should 'Cromwell' be pronounced?

Here are some pieces of evidence:

1. The village of Cromwell in early written records.

'Cromwell' was probably pronounced differently in the sixteenth century. The pronunciation of many words has changed over the years; for example tea was once pronounced 'tay' and obliged, 'obleeged'. Today, villagers in Cromwell pronounce it 'Crumwell', and if you look at the table below you can see that this is probably not new.

Date	Record	Village name
1086	DOMESDAY BOOK. An enquiry into every village and town for William the Conqueror	CRUNWELLE
1186	PIPE ROLL. A yearly record of money paid to the Exchequer	CRUMWELLA
1230	PIPE ROLL.	CRUMBWELL

2. Thomas Cromwell's signature.

Both read 'Thomas Crumwell'. The top one is from a letter to Sir Thomas Wyatt in 1539 and the second is from a letter written in the Tower to Henry VIII.

In France he was called 'Cremuel' and in Italy 'Cremonello'.

3. A contemporary verse about Cromwell.

This describes him as a crumb choking people:

speck or particle

'Much ill cometh of a small *mote*,
As crumb well set in a man's throat.'

1 From this evidence, how do you think Cromwell pronounced his name?

2 Was his name always spelt the same way?

3 Today his name is always spelt 'Cromwell'. What are the reasons for doing this, do you think?

The Cromwell coat of arms

For some people, a family surname was not the full identification. The nobility identified themselves with 'coats of arms' as well. These were special patterns designed by the Royal Heralds and used on shields, armour, letter-seals, tapestries, tombs – in fact anything relating to that person. Each person had his or her own particular design, part of it inherited from the father and the other part from the mother. Elder sons had different designs from younger sons. There were also punishments for bearing arms to which you were not entitled.

Thomas Cromwell was not born noble with a title and, like most people only had a surname at first. However, when Henry VIII knighted him Sir Thomas Cromwell in 1533, he was allowed a coat of arms. A new one was therefore designed for him by the Royal Heralds.

THOMAS CROMWELL'S COAT OF ARMS, GRANTED IN 1533.

In heraldic language its blazon [description] is: 'azure, on a fess between 3 lions rampant or, a rose gules, barbed vert, between 2 Cornish choughs proper'. This means: blue background; 3 gold lions, standing up; on a stripe across the middle, a red rose with green leaves between two black Cornish choughs with red legs and bills.

Obverse (top) and reverse (below) of a silver gilt medal struck in 1538 to commemorate Cromwell's election as a Knight of the Garter. Note his coat of arms at top left and bottom right.

Baron Cromwell or Earl of Essex?

Thomas went on to become 'Baron Cromwell of Oakham' in 1536. When he was raised even higher in 1539, however, he did not want to become 'Earl Cromwell'. There had already been a family of noble Cromwells who had died out in Henry VI's reign (1422–61) and Thomas felt that it would be a mistake to use their title. He said he

> would not wear another man's coat for fear the owner thereof should pluck it off his ears.

So he became 'Thomas Cromwell, Earl of Essex'.

Some titles which the king gave were 'in perpetuity' (for ever), which meant that when the title-holder died his eldest son would inherit it, then his eldest son, and so on. Other titles were given to the holder for his lifetime only. In Thomas Cromwell's case, his son Gregory became Baron Cromwell in turn – but not Earl of Essex. That title was taken from the family when Thomas was executed.

Cultivating the family tree

In the Early Modern Age another important part of a family's identity was its genealogy, or family tree. This was not a new interest or special only to England. Why was there so much interest in family ancestry? People today are curious about their ancestors, but in the sixteenth century there were practical reasons for wanting to know.

Members of the Cromwell family would want to be sure of such things as: which was the senior branch of the family; which branch, if any, was likely to die out; which members were making good marriages, acquiring riches or had bright prospects; who stood to inherit what, whether houses, land, money, business or titles. Legal battles might result if ever there was arguing among the family and these could only cause damage because of the expense. An example of how lineage could operate was seen in the (fifteenth-century) 'Wars of the Roses'. Civil war resulted when several nobles claimed the right to the throne by different lines of descent within the family of Edward III.

People outside the Cromwell family would want to know details of their family tree for different, but equally important, reasons. If any dealings with the Cromwells were planned, such as marriage or business, an outsider would wish to know whether they were 'higher' or 'lower' than the Cromwells in society. This would affect the terms of any arrangements made as well as everyday attitudes.

Opposite is Thomas Cromwell's family tree, as far as it is known.

Thomas moved from one level of society to another during his life – just the sort of thing which would interest his family and affect the behaviour of other people towards him.

1 Read Chapter 2 'The Four Sorts' in *A World of Change*. Into which level of society was Thomas Cromwell born?

2 Was Thomas born into the senior branch of the Cromwell family?

3 Knowledge of kinship tended to be better recorded among royalty and nobility than the peasantry. Why might this be? You might be able to think of several reasons.

4 Here are some of the many special terms family historians use to describe how people are related to each other: maternal, paternal, patronymic, sibling, spouse, stepfather, godparent, first cousin, née, maiden name, ward, endogamy, primogeniture, kindred, kin, clan, tribe, dynasty, morganatic marriage, consanguinity, minor, generation. Look up their meanings in a dictionary.

5 There are many genealogies in the Old Testament of the Bible – for example Genesis, chapters 10 and 11. Who can find the longest?

6 Draw your own family tree from memory as far as you can.

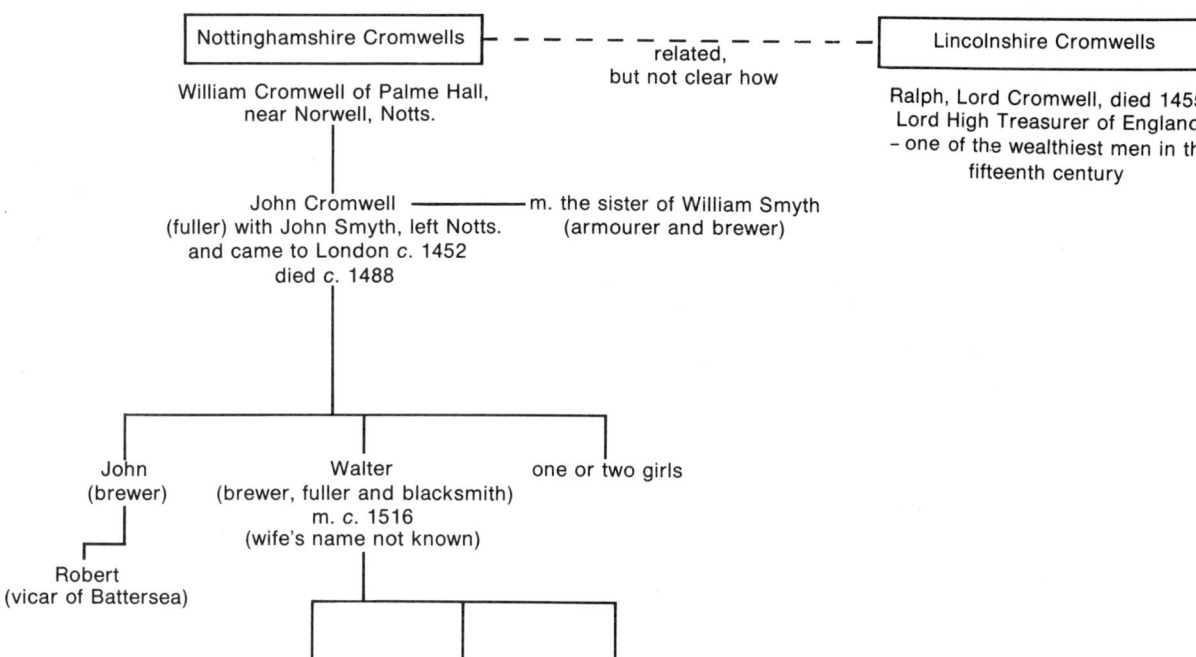

The group portrait below is a family tree in pictures. It was painted nearly 60 years after Thomas More's death and shows five generations of Mores. The picture was painted not only to preserve their likeness, but also to make the point that, despite persecution, the family was staying true to the Roman Catholic faith generation after generation. The generations are numbered above their heads.

Thomas Cromwell or Thomas Smyth?

This portrait is called 'Thomas Cromwell aged 14 in AD 1515'. After reading this page, can you say why it probably is not him?

> The Assize of Ale was a law passed to control the production and quality of locally brewed ale.

Having traced Thomas' position in his family, we can now look at the man himself more closely.

Very little is known about his early life. No documents recording his birth, schooling or apprenticeship are known, but it is thought that he was born in about 1485. As a young man he travelled and worked abroad, although there are only a few clues as to what he did and where he went.

Thomas' parents lived in Putney, which was then a village on the outskirts of London. His mother's name is not known but she originally came from Derbyshire, to join the household of a Putney lawyer. Thomas' father, Walter Cromwell, had been apprenticed as an armourer to his uncle William Smyth and was often known as 'Walter Smyth'. Walter inherited his father's fulling mill (processing woollen cloth) and built up several more businesses: as blacksmith or farrier, fuller or shearman and brewer or publican. In about 1500 he was leasing 30 acres of land which Thomas' grandfather had leased from the Lord of the Manor, but he also had the use of 90 acres in nearby Wandsworth and 'divers arable lands' in Roehampton, for which he was excused rent. In 1495 and 1496 he was Constable of Putney – a parish responsibility held in turn by the leading householders in the parish.

Walter was not, however, entirely respectable. He was charged with offences against the Assize of Ale and fined 6d. *forty eight* times between 1475 and 1501. The ale should have been officially tasted before sale to check its quality. The fine was about a week's wages for a labourer. He was often drunk and in 1477 was convicted and fined 20d. for assault and 'drawing blood'. Walter also abused his rights as a tenant, putting cattle on land he had no right to use and cutting more than his fair share of furze. Finally, in 1514 he committed a serious fraud by altering the documents of his tenancy. The Lord of the Manor's beadle reclaimed all Walter's lands and he lost his position within the parish. He died in about 1516.

Possibly, young Thomas was unruly too. The Tudor historian John Foxe, who is not always reliable, records Thomas later telling his friend Archbishop Cranmer that he had been a ruffian in his younger days. In 1535 Emperor Charles V's ambassador to England wrote that the young Thomas had been 'assez mal condicionner' – ill behaved. It is thought that he did not get on well with his father and perhaps was in trouble with the law. Around 1500, aged about 15, he left home and went abroad.

1 Suggest reasons why there is no official record of Thomas' birth.

2 Write Walter's defence of himself when he was brought to court for the forty-eighth time for offences against the Assize of Ale. What reasons might there be for continually committing the same offence?

When Thomas went overseas it is said that he became a page to a French mercenary, campaigned in Italy, and was at the battle of Garigliano in December 1503 when the Spanish defeated the French to gain control of southern Italy. Later he went to Rome, and eventually, possibly destitute and calling himself Thomas Smyth, found work in Florence with the international merchant bankers, the Frescobaldi. By 1512 he was in Antwerp, in the Netherlands, where he was both clerk to an English wool merchant and running his own cloth business.

Cromwell's years abroad mean that he must have become fluent in French, Italian and Dutch, and a sharp enough accountant to impress some shrewd people. He was also able to fend for himself, find jobs and make money, without family help – although we do not know if anyone else helped him. By the time he returned to England he must have met many men both in war-torn areas and over the business table. He would have had first-hand experience of foreign markets, economic problems and international commercial law. This was valuable experience – it made him stand out from the crowd: his familiarity with Italian thoughts, language and attitudes were the signs of a cultivated man in England, rather than just a brewer's son.

Trying to fill the gaps, and knowing what Thomas later went on to do, some historians have formed other theories about his time overseas. For instance, that he preferred the counting-house to the battlefield; that he might have encountered, and been repelled by, the corrupt behaviour of the Pope while he was in Rome; that, in Florence, he read and liked the new ideas of Niccolò Machiavelli about how princes should go about getting their own way. Nevertheless these are theories – not proven truths.

■ On a historical map of Europe find the places Thomas visited. Plan a route that he could have taken in the early sixteenth century.

Pope Julius II in 1512, the Pope when Thomas was in Italy.

Husband and father

By 1513 Thomas was father of a son, Gregory. From this we deduce that he was then back in England and married (church laws about having children before marriage were very strict, and Thomas, we know, was quite devout). When aged about 28, Thomas had married a widow, Elizabeth Wykys. This fact reveals a great deal about Tudor family life.

While the 'age of consent' was fixed by the Church (12 for girls, 14 for boys), the age at which marriages actually took place varied according to the level of society from which the couple came. Children of wealthier parents often married much younger than did Thomas Cromwell, and could be betrothed (engaged) while still infants. Wealthy parents could afford to provide land or income for their children to support the marriage. They also liked to settle as soon as possible who would inherit what in order to avoid legal problems later and to ensure that the family would not die out.

Elizabeth was a widow, Thomas her second husband. Her age is unknown. Her mother, Mercy, had also married twice; Thomas' own mother married again after Walter's death and Thomas' son Gregory married a widow. This was not unusual, as shown where statistics exist: for example, in Coventry in 1523, there were nearly nine times as many widows as widowers. Widowhood was so common because many women died in childbirth, leaving their husbands as middle-aged widowers. The men then re-married, choosing young girls who might have more children. These young wives would be likely to outlive their older husbands and become young widows.

Princess Mary aged 28 (1544). She was first betrothed at the age of two to the new-born Dauphin of France and at six to the Holy Roman Emperor, Charles V, aged 22. She married neither.

To attract a wife, Thomas would have had to have been able to support her and any children. He seems to have been an only son and might therefore expect to take over the land leases or business on the death of his father, but from what we know of Walter, perhaps this looked unlikely. His own businesses (cloth finishing, moneylending and law) must have been flourishing.

By law, when a woman married, all her property became her husband's. If he died, his widow was entitled to inherit all of his property if there were no children; a widow with children was only entitled to one third. Marrying a widow without children could be very profitable, for she would bring to the marriage both her original dowry and all her first husband's property.

Elizabeth seems to have had no previous children. She brought Thomas property from both her first husband, who had been a Yeoman of the Guard at court and from her father, John Wykys, a *shearman* (cloth-finisher) who had grown wealthy as a gentleman usher to Henry VII. Thomas took over his cloth business and employed servants to run it until about 1524.

More information about how marriages were arranged at Thomas' level of society comes from other marriages in the family. Thomas' sisters, Katherine and Elizabeth, would each have needed a dowry in order to make a good marriage. A dowry was either money or property and an account of what the girl was to inherit later, given by her father to her new husband. The better the dowry, the richer the husband a girl might expect to marry. Later, when he was rich, Thomas left money in his will for dowries for 20 poor maidens. Katherine married a Welsh lawyer called Morgan Williams. Morgan and his father had connections at Henry VII's court. Elizabeth married a sheep farmer named William Wellyfed. Wellyfed joined his business to his father-in-law's just as Thomas had done with his father-in-law. Finally, another family marriage was made when Elizabeth Wykys' sister, Joan, married one of Thomas' best friends, John Williamson.

Cromwell's wife died in 1527, perhaps from the epidemic of 'sweating sickness' in London at that time. On 12 July 1529 Thomas made his will. From this we know that there were three children: Gregory, Grace and Anne. Later the names of Grace and Anne were crossed out. Like many children at the time, they had not survived childhood. The average number of children in a family was six or seven, but more than one in five died before the age of ten and two thirds of those were in their first year. Wealthier women tended to marry earlier and have more children than poor ones, but there is some evidence to suggest that their children were less likely to survive than poorer ones. Wet-nurses were often used to breastfeed noble children and the chances of catching infection were greater.

1 Do business links seem to have anything to do with marriage? Can you form a theory about how men might have first met the women who became their wives? What advantage was there if two sisters married two friends?

2 Why would a woman want to be very sure before marrying him that a man would be able to support her?

3 Why did Welshmen have good prospects at Henry VII's court?

4 What do you think the names 'Wellyfed' and 'Smyth' refer to?

5 Do you think Walter Cromwell provided his daughters Katherine and Elizabeth with good dowries?

6 Why do you think people tended to marry people of the same rank as themselves in society?

7 A puzzle: why might parents want as many children as possible when they would be so expensive? What problems could there be if they had several sons? What problems could there be if they had several daughters?

'Trusty and right well-beloved counsellor'

Cardinal Wolsey. He holds a rod with a small crown at the top as a symbol of royal authority.

Henry VIII in about 1536

In July 1529, when he wrote his will, Thomas was moving up the career ladder quite fast and from now on information about him is more plentiful. This book deals mostly with his family life but we will look briefly at his political career to see how his life changed and why this affected his family.

On his return to England Thomas had set up various businesses as a shearman, wool dyer, moneylender and solicitor. Law was an ambitious choice: it was the most highly respected profession and the most likely to make him rich. Around 1520 he became known to Cardinal Wolsey, Henry VIII's immensely rich and powerful chief minister. In 1523 he sat in Parliament as an MP and by 1524 Thomas had entered Wolsey's service. His legal and commercial knowledge, his toughness and his huge appetite for hard work made him the ideal person to supervise the closure of several small monasteries and the building of Wolsey's new college at Oxford.

In October 1529, however, Wolsey fell from Henry VIII's favour and suddenly Cromwell's own career was in danger. As Wolsey's servant would he be disgraced too? George Cavendish, another of Wolsey's men, found Cromwell in the great chamber of the Palace of Esher on 1 November 1529. Cromwell was saying his prayers but seemed to be crying. Cavendish asked whether Wolsey was in danger, or Cromwell in trouble:

> Nay, quoth he, I am like to lose all that I have travailed for all the days of my life, for doing of my master true and diligent service.

In the event Cromwell both stayed outwardly loyal to Wolsey and avoided disgrace. But he needed a new patron and soon entered the King's service. Henry was as impressed as Wolsey had been by Cromwell's energy and abilities and over the next ten years, while Cromwell devoted himself to the royal service, rewarded him steadily with more responsibilities and greater prospects. Opposite is a diagram summarising his career and his rewards.

1 Today many people expect to do only one job at a time. Was this always the case in Thomas' time? What about his father, Walter, and his father-in-law, John? Can you think of any people who hold more than one position nowadays?

2 Make lists to show which of Cromwell's jobs were important government jobs, 'household' jobs in the palace, linked to church affairs, or concerned with the management of other people's estates.

1540	created Earl of Essex
	Steward of the late monastery of Furness
	High Steward of Reading
1539	Steward of the Honour of Reylegh and Baliff of Reylegh and the Hundred of Rochford
	Great Chamberlain of England
	Constable of Leeds Castle
1538	Master of the Mint and Keeper of Carisbrooke Park
	Constable of Carisbrooke Castle
	Steward, Surveyor, Receiver and Bailiff of the Crown lands in the Isle of Wight
	Captain of the Isle of Wight
1537	Warden and Chief Justice of the Royal forests north of the Trent
	Dean of Wells
	Steward of the Honour of Havering atte Bower and Keeper of the house, park and forest
	Knight of the Garter
1536	created Baron Cromwell of Oakham
	Keeper of the Privy Seal
	Prebendary of Blewbery
	Chief Steward of the Manor of Writtle and Keeper of the park
1535	Visitor of the University of Cambridge
	High Steward of the University of Cambridge
	Steward of the Manor of Savoy and Bailiff of Enfield
	Steward of the Manors of Edelmeton and Sayes Bery
	Chancellor of the University of Cambridge
	Visitor-General of the Monasteries
	Vicar-General and Vicegerent of the King in Spirituals
1534	Master of the Rolls, until 1536
	Joint Constable of Berkeley Castle, Keeper of the park, Master of the game, Keeper of Hynton wood and Red wood
	Principal Secretary to the King
	Joint Constable of Hertford Castle and Hertingfordbury and Keeper of the park
1533	Recorder of Bristol
	Chancellor of the Exchequer
	created Knight
1532	Master of the King's Wards
	Clerk of the Hanaper
	Master of the Jewel House
1531	Privy Councillor
1530	
1529	MP for Taunton, until 1536

Money

Cromwell's wealth increased very rapidly in the years after joining Wolsey's and then Henry's service. In 1535 his earnings for the year amounted to £4011 17s. $4\frac{1}{4}$d., three times as much money as many earls had (but Wolsey had been four or five times wealthier than Cromwell ever was). His income came from several sources, not from just one salary at a time. It was up to him to find these sources for himself. He complained

> I never had promotion by my Lord Wolsey to the increase of my living.

Cromwell's sources of income were:

1. Payments in money and kind from grateful clients and friends. For example, six plovers 'for to drink a quart of wine withal' from William Bareth in 1525 and twenty marks in 1526 from alderman George Monoux; in 1528 Richard Bellyssis promised him a good gelding if he would appoint a friend as mint-master in Durham.

2. Embezzlement or bribery. There were continual complaints about Cromwell's greed during the dissolution of the monasteries, when a wealthy abbey could pay him to treat them gently.

> No lord or gentleman in England beareth love or favour to my Lord Privy Seal because he is so great a taker of money, for he will speak, solicit or do for no man, but all for money.

3. Fees of patents, which were payments made when someone was knighted, granted lands or made other legal arrangements.

4. Profits from managing other people's estates, as steward or bailiff, for instance when the heir was too young to do so himself.

5. The rent of lands he owned in his own right. Some he bought; others he was given by the King, such as the Manor of Wimbledon which covered seven parishes, and lands from the dissolved monasteries of Lewes, St Osyth, Launde, Michelham, Modenham and Alcester.

6. Wages for royal appointments. For example, in 1535: Master of the Rolls: £284 0s. 18d.; Chancellor of the Exchequer: £651 10s.; Master of the Jewel House: £75 1s.; Clerk of the Hanaper: £58 6s. $0\frac{1}{2}$d.; High Steward of the Queen's Lands: £201.

1 Add up the wages for royal appointments in 1535. What proportion of Cromwell's total income did they represent for that year?

2 Was Cromwell greedy or not? This is a tricky question: try to think of reasons that he might use in his own defence (remembering that there was no 'welfare state') and criticisms that his attackers might bring against him.

'Master of our jewel house'
This is a close copy of a painting by Hans Holbein, a German artist working in London who Cromwell probably met when they were both dealing with a group of German merchants. What Cromwell and Holbein have chosen to include in the portrait represent messages they would like us to notice:

1 What are you meant to understand by each of the following: Turkish carpet on table, figured damask wall hangings, book, scissors and quill, papers; his style of clothing; his pose; his expression; the inscription on the paper: 'To Master Thomas Cromwell, trusty and right well-beloved counsellor and master of our jewel house'?

2 From the inscription, what would be the earliest and latest dates for this portrait?

Knowing the right people

Thomas' career owed much to his own natural ability but this alone would not have been enough. He also needed introductions to influential people who would give him work, pay him wages, and then recommend him to others. A good career relied on being noticed by the 'right' person. Important persons were besieged by people wanting a post or a favour of some sort, for themselves or someone else.

1 How do people apply for jobs today? How different is it from Thomas' time?

2 What are the good and bad points of the Tudor way of obtaining work? Was it a fair system?

It was only natural that as soon as Cromwell prospered his family and friends would expect him to help them with jobs or recommendations. By 1534 he had all the great offices of state under his control and the more people that were grateful to him, the better. Thomas was careful to make sure that his men could do the job – it would not be in his interest to recommend or employ incompetent people.

Thomas' son Gregory was the obvious choice to benefit from his father's influence, but Gregory was not very bright or ambitious. Thomas' nephew Richard Williams was much better material. He was employed by Thomas in the unpleasant, but very profitable, work of suppressing the monasteries. When, in 1536, the rebels in the revolt known as the Pilgrimage of Grace attacked Cromwell's reputation and demanded his death, Richard did his duty and rode out against the rebels. He even changed his surname to Cromwell. Cromwell wrote in July 1530 to Wolsey asking for a post in Wolsey's household for his kinsman 'Mr Doctor Carbot'. In June 1533 a cousin, Nicholas Glossop, asked Thomas to write to the Guild of Merchant Taylors who had stopped paying his pension. Cromwell did so and asked them at the same time to increase it:

to increase

a payment made every year

> And for as much as I bear good mind and favour towards him and it were more charity rather *to augment* his living rather than to diminish it or withdraw the same, specially now in his great age, when he has most need of help and succour, I heartily desire you that for my sake you will not only continue the payment of the said *annuity* for him for term of his life according to your said grant, but also ... to increase the same 13s. and 4d. more year by year.

One good turn deserves another. If the Guild complies, he writes:

> ye shall not only do the thing which may be right meritorious to you, but also right honourable for your said fellowship, and to me great pleasure. And for the same doing he [Nicholas] may hereafter do you pleasure and I shall be glad to do you pleasure or any good that I can for your fellowship at all times.

Desks like these were new in Cromwell's time. They were used for storing scissors, knives, quills and other writing materials. This one would have been expensive as it is covered with painted and gilded leather – perhaps something the King's Secretary would have enjoyed owning and using.

Cromwell allowed no argument. Not all his letters were as polite as this one. He had only a few suitable relatives to help, so the greater part of his influence was used on behalf of friends and employees from the days of his cloth and solicitor's businesses. They became ambassadors, spies, agents or clerks. As with the family, he wrote to obtain good opportunities or sort out trivial incidents for them. For example, he wrote to make sure that someone would be hospitable to the king's chief cook, Robert Hogan; to the Abbot of Netley, asking him to grant a new 60-year lease on Roydon farm near the sea at Southampton to John Cooke, as it would be convenient for Cooke's new job in the Admiralty; to obtain for John Point the mastership of a school in Cornwall; to request that Richard Salway be permitted to hold the office of Clerk of the Peace for Worcester; and so on.

Cromwell could be sure of his own importance when not only his social inferiors were petitioning him, but also people like the Duchess of Norfolk, Lord Berners and the Archbishop of York. By 1536 he needed one of his chaplains to deal with the huge number of requests.

Homes and gardens

When Cromwell first returned to England, he lived in Fenchurch Street, in the area favoured by lawyers. In about 1522 he moved to a grander house in Throgmorton Street and later took a lease from the Mercers Company for a mansion called 'Great Place' in Stepney (then a country parish east of London). He also had houses in Hackney and Islington, near London, and at Ewhurst in Hampshire and spent much time altering them to his taste. After 1532 he moved to his grandest house yet – a new mansion built for him on lands outside the city wall, previously occupied by the monastery of the Austin Friars. He knocked down many poor people's houses on the land to make room for his new building, but then, according to John Stow's Chronicle of about 1598, he wanted a bigger garden:

> He caused the pales of the gardens adjoining to the north part thereof on a sudden to be taken down; twenty-two feet to be measured forth right into the north of every man's ground; a line there to be drawn, a trench to be cast, a foundation laid, and a high brick wall to be built. My father had a garden there, and a house standing close to his south pale; this house they loosed from the ground, ere my father heard thereof; no warning was given him, nor other answer, when he spake to the surveyors of that work, but that their master Sir Thomas had commanded them so to do; no man durst go to argue the matter, but each man lost his land, and my father paid his whole rent, which was 6s. 6d. the year, for that half which was left. Thus much of mine own knowledge have I thought good to note, that the sudden rising of some men causeth them to forget themselves.

Cromwell was not the only person to behave like this. Henry VIII had done the same thing to Abbot Islip of Westminster when extending his new royal palace at Whitehall.

Because of his work load, Cromwell was often away from home staying at the royal palaces in and around Richmond or at the House of the Rolls. When he became Earl of Essex, the natural thing would have been to build a great country house on his lands outside London to advertise his wealth and taste, but this he did not have time to do before his death. Meanwhile he enjoyed furnishing his house at Austin Friars. His friend Stephen Vaughan writes to tell him that he has managed to acquire for Cromwell a globe with explanatory notes, a special iron chest which was so expensive that he hardly dares mention the cost, and one of only two specially illuminated chronicles from Antwerp. In March 1528 he also writes to say that he has put a strong chain across the gate following the robbery and murder of one of Cromwell's neighbours, 'that no man not well known may enter'.

A Tudor chest, intricately inlaid. These were used where today we would have wardrobes or chests of drawers.

When Gregory was 16, Thomas made his will. He gave instructions about how Gregory should be supported financially and educated until he was 22. At 24 he was to receive the following, which gives a glimpse of the household furnishings – handsome if not luxurious:

> £200 of lawful English money; 3 of my best feather beds with their bolsters; 2 of the best pairs of blankets of fustian; my best coverlet of tapestry; my quilt of yellow turkey satin; 10 pairs of my best sheets; 4 pillows of down with 4 pairs of the best pillow cases; 4 of my best table cloths; 4 of my best towels; 2 dozen of my finest napkins; 2 dozen of my other napkins; 2 garnish of my best vessell; 3 of my best brass pots; 3 of my best brass pans; 2 of my best kettles; 2 of my best spits; my best joined bed of Flanders work with the best *syler* and *tester* and other appurtenances thereto belonging; my best *press* carven of Flanders work; 6 joined stools of Flanders work; 6 of my best cushions; a basin with a lewer *parcell gilt*; my best salt gilt; my best cup gilt; 3 of my best goblets gilt; 3 other of my best goblets parcell gilt; 12 of my best silver spoons; 3 of my best drinking ale pots gilt.

headboard
canopy above a four poster bed; chest
partly gilt

In the event, the will was pointless and the great house demolished after Thomas' execution.

Bringing up Gregory

We do not know what sort of education Thomas had but as the son of a tradesman he might have been sent to school to learn reading, writing, maths and Latin, if Walter was willing to pay for it, and following that, apprenticed to a trade until his early twenties. For Gregory, however, growing up as the son of a wealthy, successful man, education meant a personal tutor at Cambridge University. He was sent there after his mother's death along with his cousin Christopher Wellyfed and several other boys, all at Cromwell's expense.

The tutor's name was John Chekyng. He sent regular reports to Cromwell: Christopher was bright enough, but Gregory was rather dull and quite hard work to teach. Cromwell seems to have thought that Chekyng was not working Gregory hard enough and did not always pay the bills for Gregory's board, lodging and tuition. Chekyng wrote complaining that he might at least pay for the damage Christopher had caused; he:

> did hinge a candle in a plate to look upon his book and so fell asleep and the candle fell into the bedstraw and burnt the bed, bolster, three overlaids and a *sparver*.

canopy above a bed

In April 1533 Gregory was taken from Cambridge and sent to live with a friend of his father's to spend the summer hunting – an aristocratic pursuit. In 1535 he came of age and moved into public life. In 1539 he was summoned to Parliament, to the House of Lords, and was among a group of courtiers who went to Calais to meet Henry's future wife, Anne of Cleves. He and his cousin Richard were champion jousters in the royal tournaments.

His father Thomas was clearly ambitious to establish the family in their new position in society. When lands were granted to him, he requested that they were either made jointly to him and Gregory, or to be inherited by Gregory at Thomas' death. Another obvious method was to link the Cromwells with nobility by marriage. Thomas never attempted this for himself, although there were unpleasant rumours about him wanting to marry Princess Mary, but for Gregory he arranged a marriage with Elizabeth Seymour, Queen Jane Seymour's sister, in August 1537.

■ What reasons might there be for Thomas not marrying a second time?

Queen Jane Seymour, Gregory's sister-in-law. She died in October 1537.

A portrait of an unknown lady from the Cromwell family, aged 21 in about 1535–40. Evidence of wealth in the family are her clothes, being able to afford a portrait and being at court where Holbein worked. The portrait was first recorded in the possession of Oliver Cromwell, a descendant, in the 1650s. She is possibly Queen Jane Seymour's sister, Elizabeth, who married Thomas Cromwell's son Gregory in 1537. Being related to royalty is, of course, another example of the Cromwells' success. After Gregory's death she married again – her third husband.

Traitors and gentlemen

Thomas Howard, 3rd Duke of Norfolk in about 1538–40. He holds the gold baton of Earl Marshal and the white staff of the Lord Treasurer.

As Cromwell entered the council chamber after dinner on 10 June 1540, he was stunned to hear the Duke of Norfolk shout: 'Cromwell, do not sit there, traitors do not sit with gentlemen'.

Immediately the guard entered and arrested Cromwell in the King's name, charging him with treason. Cromwell realised that he was in a trap planned by his enemies and that now they, not he, had the King's favour. Hostility between Cromwell on one side, and Norfolk and Bishop Stephen Gardiner on the other, had been simmering for years. Cromwell had always outwitted them and avoided open argument. Now, however, when Henry was blaming Cromwell for the unsatisfactory marriage with Anne of Cleves, Norfolk and Gardiner had seized their chance to pay him back for previous defeats. Cromwell knew that there would be no way out. Death was the penalty for treason. He pleaded for a quick end. Norfolk could not resist enjoying his victory. He tore the insignia of St George from around Cromwell's neck and the Earl of Southampton, previously a friend, ripped the Garter from him. Thomas was taken by barge along the Thames to the Tower of London.

From his cell in the Tower Thomas wrote letters to Henry, pleading for mercy, still not knowing the exact charge against him. In this extract Thomas' own spelling and punctuation have been kept:

> Your Maiestye hathe bene the most bountyffull prynce to me that euer was kying to his Subiect ye and more lyke a dere Father your Magestye not offended then a maister. Such hathe bene your most graue and godlye counsayles towardes me at sundrye tymes in that I haue offended I ax your mercye.

He said that he had only tried to serve, strengthen and enrich Henry and that he was not guilty of several things people had wrongly accused him of. But he would never be able to explain everything:

> Neuertheles Sir I haue medelyd in So many matyers vnder your Highnes that I am not able to answer them all but one thing I am well assuryd off that wittinglye and willinglye I haue not hadde will to offend your Highnes but harde it ys for me or any other medlyng as I haue done to lyue vnder your grace and your lawse but we must daylye offende and wher I haue offendyd, I most humlye aske mercye and pardon at your gracyous will and plesure.

From Henry there was no pardon, although he asked for one letter to be read out three times. Archbishop Cranmer pleaded with him, saying that if Henry could not trust Cromwell, whom could he trust? Both knew that many people, rich and poor, were glad to see Cromwell go. Only those 'who knew nothing but truth by him both lamented him and heartily prayed for him'. Cromwell's agents, servants and other employees could not save him for, like him, they were mostly 'new men' without great influence. They would also be keen to escape the disaster and re-attach themselves to a patron with better prospects, as Thomas had done when Wolsey fell. In fact, the only protection was to have the King's favour.

Evidence against Cromwell was gathered. Sir Richard Rich and Sir George Throgmorton swore in Parliament that Cromwell had said words treasonable under the 1534 Treason Act. On 29 June, Cromwell was condemned as a traitor by Act of Attainder. In other words, the Lords and Commons heard the evidence and voted that he was guilty; Cromwell was not allowed to speak in his own defence. From the day of his arrest and in the Attainder, he was stripped of all his titles and called 'Thomas Cromwell, shearman'.

Thomas Cranmer, Archbishop of Canterbury.

The charges against Cromwell were that:

1. He had given the King bad advice.
2. His methods of administration had been corrupt and illegal.
3. He had been too lenient in justice, particularly to heretics.
4. He had encouraged heretical religious beliefs and had said that he himself would stand by these beliefs even if it meant fighting the King to defend them.
5. He had acted for personal gain and maintained too large a household.
6. He 'disdained' the other nobles; in other words, did not treat them with enough respect. He had once said that 'if the lords would handle him so, that he would give them such a breakfast as never was made in England'.
7. He had plans to marry the Princess Mary and make himself King.
8. He had betrayed Henry's confidences about the marriage to Anne of Cleves.

Heretic
One whose beliefs differ from the official teaching of the Church.

1 After the Treason Act of 1534, it was treason to say that the king was a tyrant or a heretic. Which of the charges listed above would be treasonable? Why do you think there were so many charges?

2 Which of the charges show jealousy of Cromwell's success?

3 Considering the things Cromwell had done during his time in power, would you support his attackers or his defenders in June 1540?

4 If you were Cromwell, pleading for your life, what arguments would you use to Henry? Which of your arguments do you think would have the most effect on him and which the least?

5 Margaret Pole, Countess of Salisbury. Cromwell had worked for her death by Act of Attainder; by another Attainder, in 1539, he brought about the conviction of 53 people. What were the dangers and benefits of this method compared to trial by jury?

After the Act of Attainder, Thomas still pleaded for mercy, although he doubtless knew that there would be none. His other hope was for a quick end, but Henry delayed the execution for a further seven weeks. He needed Cromwell's evidence to secure the divorce from Anne of Cleves. Once this had been finalised, the execution took place on Tower Green on 29 July. At the last moment he was spared the slow death by hanging, drawing and quartering, which his lowered status ('shearman') should have earned, but was allowed the 'mercy' of execution by beheading. After the execution, his final speech was printed and publicly circulated. His head was placed on a stake on London Bridge with those of other traitors.

A man of base estate

Two hours after Cromwell was arrested, soldiers entered his house at Austin Friars and removed all its contents to the Treasury, even though nothing had yet been proved against him. Traitors' property was always confiscated by the Crown. Onlookers were apparently surprised at how little wealth Cromwell had, although

> it was far too much for one of his sort. The money was £7,000 and the silver plate, including crosses, chalices and other spoils of the church, might be as much more.

'Far too much for one of his sort'? This was one of the biggest complaints against Cromwell. It was a prejudice against people climbing from one level of society to another. However much Cromwell tried to live like a dignified lord and avoid vulgar show, people never forgot his origins: as he remarked wryly at his execution, his humble birth was 'not unknown to some of you'. Even his friend, Sir Thomas Eliot, wrote:

> it was excellent virtue and learning that enabled a man of base estate of the commonality to be thought worthy to be so much advanced.

It was believed that people such as Cromwell were attempting to destroy the proper ranks of society, which God had created. People at all levels thought this; it was not just the nobility complaining that he was pushing in where he was not wanted. There was very little defence against it.

A lion's strength

Did Thomas fear the ruin of his son Gregory as well as himself? Probably. His last speech on the scaffold stressed that he alone was guilty. Luckily Gregory remained in favour, perhaps because of his marriage into the royal family. The title of Baron Cromwell and the Cromwell lands, which Thomas had forfeited in the Attainder, were re-granted to Gregory just five months later, on 18 December 1540, but the great house at Austin Friars was pulled down. Thomas' nephew, Richard Cromwell (formerly Williams), dared to go about in open mourning for his uncle, but he too remained in Henry's favour, as you will see in the next chapter. The family tree shows that the family continued to make good marriages and retain their new position in society without any political influence.

Henry saw no reason to harm Cromwell's servants and many of them were re-employed in 1540, just as Wolsey's servants had been in 1529.

Six months later Norfolk was in turn banished from court and Henry had begun to regret Cromwell's death:

> On light pretexts, by false accusation they made me put to death the most faithful servant I have ever had...

But was Henry sorry for Cromwell or sorry for himself? Earlier, Wolsey and More had both followed the same path as Cromwell. They learnt the danger. More said:

> rather than he will either miss or want any part of his will or appetite, he will put the loss of one half of his kingdom in danger.... I warn you to be well advised and assured what matter ye put in his head for ye shall never put it out again.

Wolsey said:

> If you will follow my poor advice, you shall, in your counsel giving unto his Grace ever tell him what he ought to do, but never what he is able to do.... For if a lion knew his own strength, hard were it for any man to rule him.

Sir Thomas More in about 1528. Like Cromwell, he too fell from Henry's favour and was executed.

1 In what ways did Cromwell's family life alter as he became more important?

2 Think of some of the differences between sixteenth-century family life and ours today.

3 Write an entry for Gregory's diary on the day of Thomas' execution. What would his thoughts be?

The Cromwell family 1540–1640

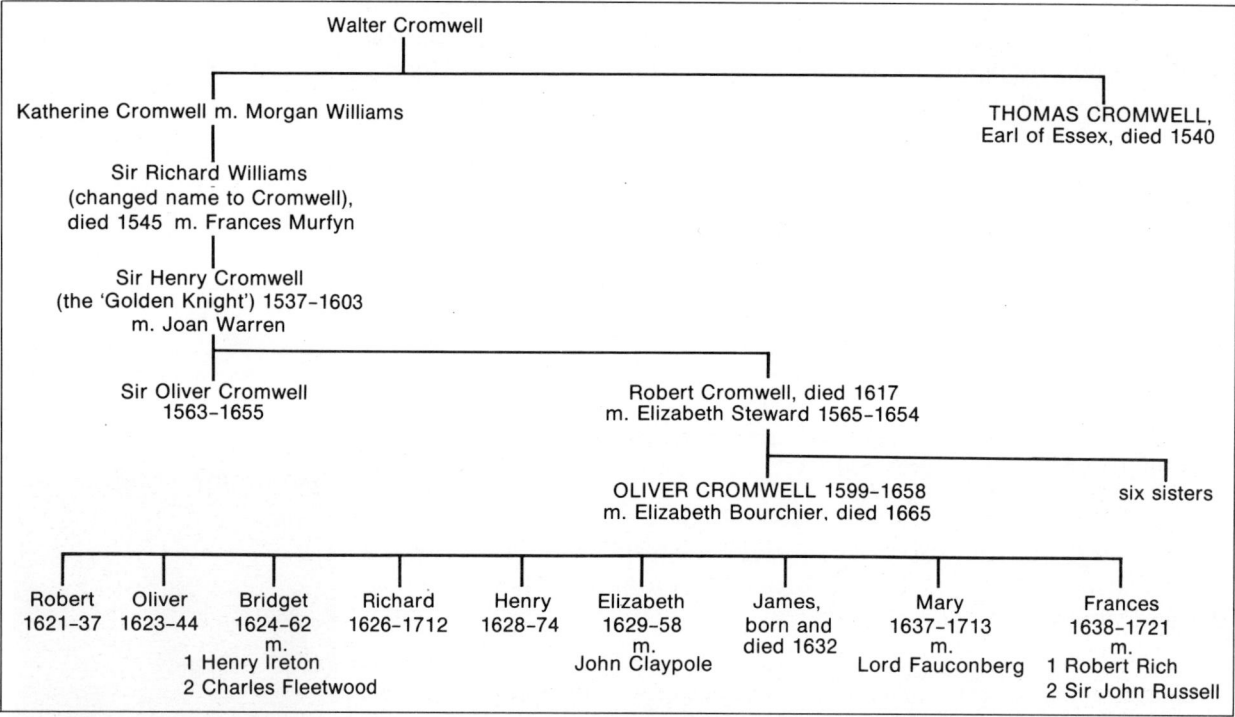

This family tree makes clear the link between Thomas and Oliver Cromwell. All Oliver's children are shown, but not Thomas' direct descendants.

The story of the Cromwell Family between 1540 and 1640 is an excellent example of how family fortunes could be made in the service of royalty. This chapter will tell you more about this. It will also explain where Oliver Cromwell fits into the family picture and describe his first 40 years of life, before he became an important national figure.

In 1494 Katherine, the daughter of the prosperous Putney tradesman Walter Cromwell, married Morgan Williams, the son of a Welsh archer who had grown rich in the service of Henry VII. They had a son, Richard, a sturdy, intelligent boy who developed into an ambitious young man. This was the person who was useful to his powerful uncle Thomas Cromwell in the tough job of dissolving the monasteries and redistributing their lands. Richard Williams was a loyal and efficient worker for his uncle. He was well rewarded, receiving money and grants of land in the Huntingdon area, particularly the estates of the former monastery at Hinchingbrooke.

Dick Williams becomes Sir Richard Cromwell

These lands were given him in the name of Richard Cromwell not Richard Williams. King Henry VIII had noticed this energetic man, and suggested he take the family name of his famous uncle. Family surnames were not really fixed at that time, so Richard Williams had no objection to becoming Richard Cromwell. The King greatly approved of him. Richard was a strong character with the sort of personal style that Henry liked – fine horses, rich clothes, skill at jousting. Raphael Holinshed, in his Chronicles of England, first published in 1577, mentions him:

> On May Day (1540) was a great triumph of jousting at Westminster, which joust had been proclaimed in France, Flanders, Scotland and Spain, for all comers that would against the challengers of England: which were Sir John Judleie, Sir Thomas Seimer, Sir Thomas Poinings, Sir George Carew, knights, Anthonie Kingston, and Richard Cromwell, esquires, which said challengers came into the lists that day richly apparelled, and their horses trapped all in white velvet

The meeting of Henry VIII and the Emperor Maximilian in 1513. Henry has a guard of honour of skilful jousters.

Richard was so successful in this jousting team that the King knighted him, saying, as several historians have written: 'Formerly thou wast my Dick, but hereafter shalt be my Diamond.' Certainly Sir Richard Cromwell was valuable to Henry, who gave him more land and money, made him a general during the war with France in 1543, and appointed him High Sheriff of Huntingdonshire and Cambridgeshire. This was a success story: from clever Welsh boy to favoured courtier and local figure. The fall and execution of his famous uncle in 1540 did not affect his rise to power and influence. He had the King's favour and held it until he died in 1546.

The Golden Knight

Sir Richard's estates passed to his son Henry, who built himself a house at Hinchingbrooke, in Huntingdonshire. This completed the success story of this branch of the Cromwells. The house was a centre of local politics and a place to display wealth and good connections by entertaining important people. Queen Elizabeth I knighted Henry, and stayed with him on one of her 'progresses' around the country. Sir Henry Cromwell, like his father, was a glamorous public figure, whom people called the 'Golden Knight'.

This is either Sir Henry Cromwell or Sir Oliver; probably the former, according to the Cromwell Museum at Huntingdon.

The first Oliver

The eldest son of Sir Henry was the first Oliver Cromwell we meet. He too was knighted by Queen Elizabeth. Realising that royal favour was the key to his family's fortune, he worked hard to impress Elizabeth's successor, James I. In 1603 when James travelled from Scotland to London to inherit the English throne, he was magnificently entertained at Hinchingbrooke, as the historian John Nichols reported:

fast
various

> His Majesty had such entertainment as the like had not been seen in any place before since his first setting forward out of Scotland. There was such plenty and variety of meats, such diversity of wines, and those not riff-raff, but ever of the best kind, and the cellers open at any man's pleasure.... Also Master Cromwell presented his Majesty with many rich and respectable gifts, as a very great, and a very fair wrought standing cup of gold, goodly horses, *fleet* and deep-mouthed houndes, *divers* hawks of excellent wing, and at the remove gave fifty pounds amongst his Majesty's Officers.

James I was impressed with such lavish hospitality and made several more costly (to Sir Oliver!) visits. Sir Oliver was 'investing' in the monarchy, hoping to receive his interest in land, jobs or money.

James, however, had other favourites, and nothing came to the Cromwells. Sir Oliver had miscalculated: possibly he was too cultured and civilised for the coarse-minded monarch or not tough or clever enough to impress the King's advisors. Sadly, he had to sell Hinchingbrooke to the Montague family, and go and live in one of his smaller houses. As a result the local power and prestige of the Cromwells was greatly reduced.

1 No portrait of Richard Williams/Cromwell survives. Make your own.

2 Make up a conversation between Sir Oliver and his wife about the need to sell Hinchingbrooke House.

3 What would be some of the chapter headings for a book called 'How to Succeed in Tudor England'?

Oliver Cromwell: the future Lord Protector

The Oliver Cromwell who became Lord Protector was the nephew of the unfortunate Sir Oliver Cromwell. Sir Oliver's brother Robert, an altogether quieter and more modest individual who had inherited a small estate near Huntingdon from the 'Golden Knight', was the father of the future national leader. Robert's wife, Elizabeth Steward, was also from a family whose money came from former monastic lands.

Oliver was born on 25 April 1599. Little definite is known about his boyhood, although many stories unsupported by evidence have been told in history books. For example, that when aged four he was taken to Hinchingbrooke House to meet James I and his family. He quarrelled with little Prince Charles (later King Charles I) and punched his nose. A good story, but *not* good history!

This may be Oliver as a boy. The evidence to prove it does not exist.

Robert Cromwell, Oliver's father. Briefly an MP (in 1593), he preferred a quiet life as a country gentleman.

Elizabeth Cromwell, Oliver's mother. She lived to see her son become the greatest man in Britain. Their relationship was warm and strong.

Education

Oliver was sent to the Free School at Huntingdon. The Headmaster was Dr Thomas Beard, a well-known Puritan preacher and writer whose book *The Theatre of God's Judgements* had come out in 1597. This book, and Dr Beard's teaching, introduced 12-year-old Oliver to a fierce God. This God was stern, all-seeing and a vigorous punisher of sinners, whether humble men or kings who taxed their people too much. In the struggle against sin, the 'elect' or the 'godly' were God's allies – certain of victory if they kept God's laws. This made a strong impression on Oliver's mind.

At school he also learned Latin, Greek, mathematics and history, all of which prepared him to go to Cambridge University, when he was 17.

It was normal for gentlemen's sons to be students so young. His college was Sidney Sussex, well known for its Puritan ideas. He was only there for a year because his father died in 1617 and Oliver went home to help his mother. Was he a good student? We have very little evidence, but what there is suggests that he generally preferred exercise and action to study. The historian Heath, for example, writing in 1663, and no supporter of Cromwell, said:

> During his short residence there ... he was more famous for his exercises in the Fields than in the Schools ... being one of the chief match-makers and players at Foot-ball, Cudgels or any other boysterous sport or game.

Although critical, this is probably quite accurate. He was never a great thinker about abstract ideas; he always preferred positive action and a practical, problem-solving approach.

1 What do you think were some of the questions young Oliver asked Dr Beard about God?

2 Write a letter from Oliver's tutor at Cambridge, Richard Howlet, to his father Robert Cromwell, commenting on his progress.

Farmer and local politician, 1617–40

There is, once again, little hard evidence for Oliver's life until his marriage in 1620. Most historians, however, whether for him or against him, have agreed **a)** that he was fond of drinking, games and good company and **b)** that he went to London to study law, probably at Lincoln's Inn. On 22 August 1620, he married Elizabeth Bourchier, the daughter of a rich businessman, a sensible marriage for a minor landowner. By 1638 they had nine children. Respectable, but not wealthy, he settled down to farm his estate and be a responsible local citizen. It was natural that he should become a Member of Parliament sooner or later: his father, uncle, grandfather and great-grandfather had been. He was elected an MP for Huntingdon for the 1628 Parliament, thereby restoring some of the family's prestige lost by the financial ruin of his uncle, Sir Oliver. He joined a group of MPs, many of them his relations, who opposed strongly the religious and financial policies of King Charles I. The King dissolved the Parliament quickly and ruled without one for the next 11 years.

Back in Huntingdon, Oliver became more involved in local politics and won a reputation for fierce, frequently rude, speeches in favour of the rights and traditions of the local people. His personal life went through several major difficulties, although we do not know fully what they were about. Possibly he thought of emigrating, before renting a farm near St Ives, a real

Elizabeth Cromwell, née Bourchier, by Samuel Cooper, 1651.

come-down for a land *owner*. In 1636, however, he moved to Ely where his wife's uncle had left them substantial estates. His financial position was now secure, but personal tragedy struck when his eldest son Robert died in 1637, aged 16.

This sadness, and general doubts about his purpose in life, caused a severe attack of what we would now call 'depression'. He fought it hard, and cured himself by prayer and by dedicating his life to God; as he described in a letter to his cousin Mrs St John on 13 October 1638.

> Yet to honour God by declaring what He hath done for my Soul. . . . Truly, then, this I find: that He giveth springs in a dry and barren wilderness where no water is . . . He hideth not His face from me. He giveth me to see light in His light: One beam in a dark place hath exceeding much refreshment in it. Blessed be His name for shining upon so dark a heart as mine! You know what my manner of life hath been. Oh! I lived in and loved darkness and hated the light. I was a chief, the Chief of Sinners. This is true: I hated godliness, yet God had mercy on me. O the riches of His mercy!

Oliver Cromwell by Samuel Cooper. Painted in 1649. There is no earlier picture of Cromwell that is genuine.

These are the passionate words, the authentic voice of Oliver Cromwell.

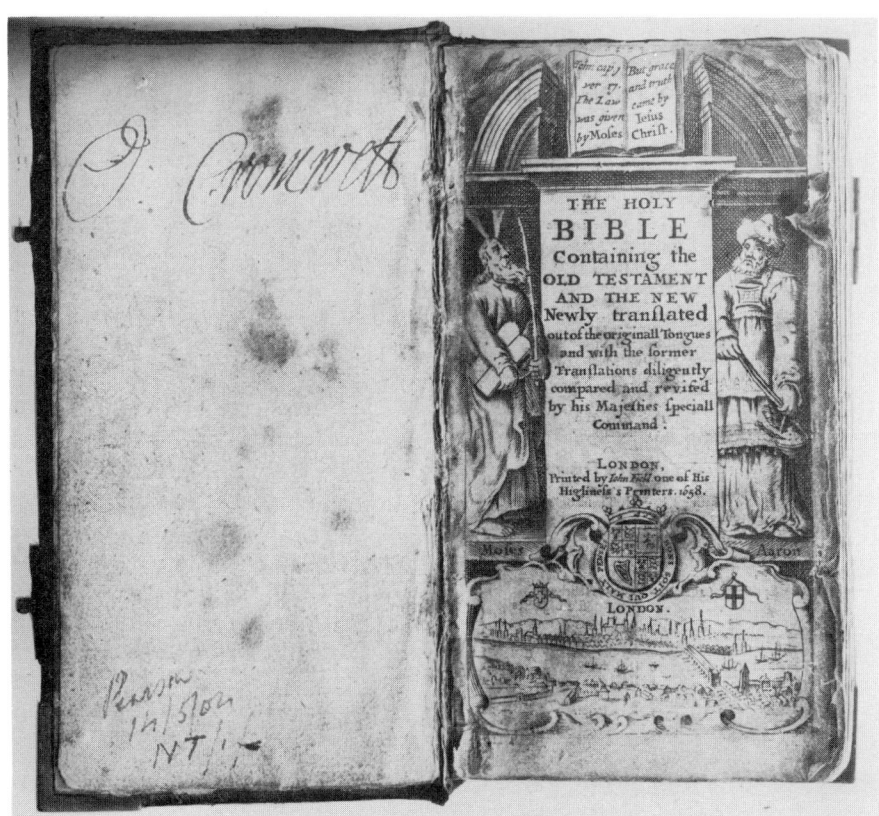

This bible was used by Oliver Cromwell.

29

Ironsides

Lord Digby, meeting John Hampden outside the House of Commons in November 1640, asked him about a large untidy man walking down some steps. Hampden replied:

> That slovenly fellow which you see before us, who hath no ornament in his speech; I say that sloven if we should come to have a breach with the King (which God forbid) in such a case will be one of the greatest men in England.

John Hampden was right. Just over nine years later, Oliver Cromwell was the ruler of Britain, having vigorously worked for the King's defeat in battle, and then his trial and execution.

In the 'Short' and 'Long' Parliaments of 1640–42 he was among a group of MPs who shared certain interests. All were landowners, many also lawyers and merchants who were fully aware of the financial problems which Charles' government was causing England, and of the legal arguments involved. Their religious beliefs were Puritan. This meant that some (like Oliver) opposed church control by regional bishops and preferred a system of self-governing 'independent' congregations. (They became known as 'Independents'). Others called themselves 'Presbyterians'. Presbyterians *did* believe in a clear-cut organisation, although not by bishops, and felt that the beliefs and services of the Church of England were becoming far too like the 'poisonous Popish ceremonies' of the Roman Catholics. Finally, there was a very strong family link among Cromwell's fellow MPs. He had 17 relatives in the 1640 Parliaments, and another nine joined later. His most politically experienced relations were his cousins John Hampden and Oliver St John, who had both opposed the King since 1627 and gone to prison for refusing to lend him money.

From November 1640, Oliver Cromwell MP gradually became more noticed. He spoke out against the government in defence of men such as John Lilburne who had been whipped and imprisoned for criticising the Church. He supported the 'Grand Remonstrance', an attack on royal policies passed by Parliament in November 1641, and was one of the first to organise preparations for war.

Oliver St John, another of Cromwell's close political friends. During the war Cromwell often wrote to him for money.

1 What punishments could befall people who criticised Charles' government? Find out in *A World of Change* and other textbooks what happened to Pym, Hampden, St John, Lilburne, Prynne, Bastwick and Richard Chambers.

2 Write a letter from one of the King's supporters in the House of Commons, warning Charles I about the new member for Cambridge (Cromwell).

30

The lovely company

In July 1642 when the King declared war, Cromwell was 42 years old, a middle-aged member of Parliament. He had never been a soldier. Three years later, he was a famous general, second-in-command of the victorious Parliamentarian New Model Army and an expert in the recruitment, training and leadership of cavalry in battle. How did he achieve this?

His background and character gave him a good start. Landowners needed to manage men and money on their estates and to know about horses – useful knowledge for a cavalry officer. He read military textbooks and accounts of battles in the Thirty Years War, then taking place in central Europe. Above all, he was sure that he was carrying out the Will of God. Each success strengthened this belief. His natural energy and force of character supplied the action. 'Up and be doing' he would say, and few could stay idle for long!

On 23 October 1642 a battle was fought at Edgehill, near Kineton in Warwickshire. Cromwell, it seems, arrived a little late for the conflict, but not too late for him to learn a very important lesson about why the Parliamentarian cavalry had done so badly against the Royalist cavalry made up of gentlemen. He told his cousin John Hampden that the Parliamentarians needed men:

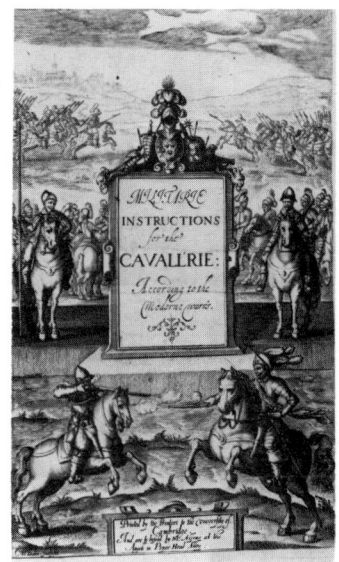

The title page of a military textbook by John Cruso.

> of a spirit that is likely to go on as far as a gentleman will go, or else I am sure you will be beaten still.

Cromwell began to put his ideas for improvement into practice during the spring of 1643. He was promoted to Colonel in the Army of the Eastern Association commanded by the Earl of Manchester, and given a commission to recruit horsemen. By April 1644 he had about 1,400 men under his personal command.

He chose religious 'godly' men who would fight for what they believed; men who had 'the root of the matter' in them, as he put it. To Cromwell, a 'godly' man was not only very religious, he was also someone who had been chosen already by God for eventual salvation, so his life on earth was thus directed to serving God. It was obvious to Cromwell that such men should be the main striking force of his fight against a King whose advisors were *not* following the true path to God. It did not matter that they were farmers, tradesmen, brewery workers, cobblers or 'such as have filled dung carts'.

As Richard Baxter, no friend of Cromwell, remarked:

> These men were of greater understanding than common soldiers ... and making not money but that which they took for *public felicity* to be their end, they were the more engaged to be valiant.

public good

Cromwell's recruiting methods may have been unusual (even alarming), but they worked. His men soon gained a reputation for remarkably good discipline because the godly soldiers, as you might expect, were generally well-behaved.

1 Draw up the application form that Cromwell might use when recruiting his soldiers. What information about a man would he want to know?

2 Cromwell selected many men of low social rank to be officers. Discuss who might object to this, and why.

'It hath pleased God...'

By 1643, Cromwell had had local military success in East Anglia by demonstrating the success of his military methods. In 1644, he became more widely known because of his contribution to the major victory at the battle of Marston Moor near York, 3 July 1644, which gave Parliament control of the north. Much of the credit for the victory was given to Cromwell. His cavalry were on the left wing. They drove off their opponents, resisted the temptation to pursue too vigorously, and were thus able to charge again and drive off more Royalist cavalry. The Royalist foot-soldiers, outnumbered by their enemies and now unprotected by cavalry, were killed where they stood: 'God made them as stubble to our swords', as Cromwell said in a letter to his cousin Valentine Walton. Sadly, in the same letter he had to tell Walton that his son had been killed. Cromwell's own second son, another Oliver, had died of disease while on active service, so he knew what the Waltons would feel.

Oliver Cromwell. This print shows him as a victorious soldier.

breathe · Sir, you know my trials this way; but the Lord supported me with this: that the Lord took him into the happiness we all *pant* and live for. There is your precious child full of glory, to know sin nor sorrow anymore.

This is an imaginary picture of Cromwell at Marston Moor in 1644. It was painted by John Ward in the early nineteenth century.

During the remainder of 1644, Cromwell and his military and political allies grew dissatisfied with the way the war was going. Cromwell quarrelled openly with his own commanding officer, the cautious Earl of Manchester. He thought Manchester was avoiding bringing the Royalists to total defeat. In an argument between Cromwell and Manchester at a Council of War we can see their differences. Manchester doubts that complete victory will help them:

> If we beat the King 99 times, he would be King still and his *posterity*, and we subjects still, but if he beat us but once we should be hanged and our posterity undone.

descendants

Cromwell thought this was admitting defeat before starting:

> My Lord, if this be so, why did we take up arms at first? This is against fighting hereafter. If so, let us make peace, be it never so base.

The final outcome of the quarrel was the 'Self-Denying Ordinance', passed through both Houses of Parliament by 3 April 1645. Briefly, this said that members of the Lords and Commons could not hold military commands and should resign them within 40 days. Manchester was forced to resign. Should not Cromwell also leave the army?

1 Write a letter from the Earl of Manchester to his friend Robert Crawford, in which the Earl gives his side of the quarrel with Cromwell, and expresses his feelings on losing it.

2 Discuss Cromwell's reasons for backing the 'Self-Denying Ordinance'.

The Earl of Manchester. Cromwell criticised his ability to lead effectively. This silver badge was produced in 1643.

The New Model Army

Having removed Manchester, and other leading generals, the way was clear for a total reorganisation of Parliament's forces. Cromwell became one of the chief organisers of the 'New Model Army', which was ready for action by May 1645. The Commander-in-Chief was Sir Thomas Fairfax, recommended by Cromwell who had fought alongside him in 1643–4. Fairfax was not political, but an experienced military commander. The job of commander of the cavalry (ranked as Lieutenant-General) was not filled straightaway. Cromwell was the obvious choice, but, as an MP, he no longer qualified.

Fairfax and the army could neither find a replacement, nor do without him. Cromwell's skill and experience were indispensable, so an exception was made for this exceptional man. Once again, the horsemen he trained played a leading part in the total defeat of the King at the battle of Naseby on 14 June 1645. After this the New Model Army marched down to the West Country where Royalist resistance continued. In a victorious campaign the professional Parliamentarians crushed the demoralised, ill-equipped Royalist forces. In June 1646 the first phase of the Civil War was over: the King had surrendered to Parliament's allies, the Scots.

Sir Thomas Fairfax. A fine soldier and Cromwell's superior officer until 1650.

Lord-General and Lord Protector

Oliver Cromwell by Robert Walker. Walker was the official painter of the leading Parliamentarians. He modelled his style on the great Sir Anthony van Dyck.

Denzil Holles was the leader of Parliament in its quarrel with the Army.

On Friday 16 December 1653, Oliver Cromwell accepted the title of Lord Protector of England, Scotland and Ireland. For the next five years until his death on 3 September 1658, he was Head of State, with all the prestige and something of the power of a king. How had he reached that position in the years following the Battle of Naseby? It is a complicated story, so we shall take it in four stages.

Stage 1 Cromwell, Parliament and the Army, 1647

Cromwell officially left the Army in July 1646. During the winter of 1646–7 he was ill and could not attend Parliament. While he was away a serious quarrel developed between Parliament and the Army. Most of the soldiers were Independents who had fought for the right to be so. They feared that Parliament was threatening their religious freedom. Furthermore, Parliament owed the Army up to 43 weeks pay. The soldiers became increasingly uncooperative, so Parliament refused to pay them. Cromwell was then sent by Parliament to negotiate with the soldiers. Once among them, he became convinced of the righteousness of their arguments and he acted as their main spokesman against Parliament. Nobody gave in, so Cromwell and the Army, having seized the King from Parliament's control, marched into London in August 1647. The Presbyterian leaders of Parliament ran away, leaving the Army and Independents in control. So in stage 1, Cromwell becomes the Army's political leader.

Stage 2 Cromwell and The Man of Blood, 1648–January 1649

The King was the problem now. He had escaped from the Army's custody, but was soon recaptured. However, his supporters in Scotland, Wales and south-eastern England were ready to fight for him again. Cromwell called him 'an obstinate man, whose heart God had hardened' and in April 1648 a 'Resolution of the Army' said

> It was our duty, if ever the Lord brought us back again in peace to call Charles Stuart, that man of blood, to account for the blood he had shed, and mischief he had done to his utmost.

Cromwell went back to war to defeat Charles Stuart, not to destroy the idea of monarchy.

While Fairfax dealt with the Royalists in the South-East, Cromwell marched to Wales with the rest of the New Model Army, defeated the Royalists at Pembroke on 11 July, then moved rapidly to the north. The Scots were invading and by 17 August had reached Preston, where Cromwell defeated them after a well-organised campaign. To Cromwell, these latest victories were, naturally, a sign of God's Providence.

> His presence hath been amongst us and by the light of his *countenance* have we *prevailed*.

face
won

Cromwell now became the force behind the plans and arrangements for the trial of the King. Fairfax was unhappy with the idea, but Cromwell had the prestige and personal drive to see it through. To one objector he said

> I tell you we will cut off his head with the Crown upon it

A German print of the execution of the King outside the Banqueting House, Whitehall.

When some of the judges hesitated to sign the warrant for the King's execution, Cromwell used strong persuasion to get their signatures. The King was executed on 30 January 1649. In stage 2, further startling success as a general increased Cromwell's influence. He used that to good effect to bring the King to trial. Once convinced that the King must be removed, his force of character was irresistible.

■ Sir Thomas Fairfax and others objected to the King's trial. Why? What do you think Cromwell said to persuade them it was necessary?

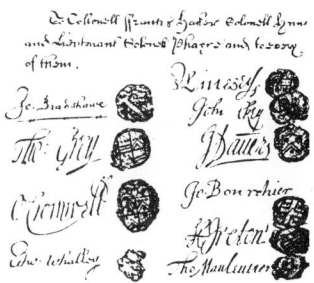

A section of the death warrant of King Charles I, showing Cromwell's signature.

35

Cromwell, the Army and the Levellers, 1647-9

Many of the ordinary soldiers, and several senior officers, were influenced by the political ideas of the Levellers, whose leader was John Lilburne. They believed that the ordinary people who had helped to win the war should have a say in whatever new government was going to be set up. As Colonel Thomas Rainsborough said

> The poorest he that is in England hath a life to live as well as the greatest he, and therefore, truly, Sir, I think it clear that every man who is to live under a government, ought first by his own consent, to put himself under that government.

We would agree with that nowadays, but in the mid-seventeenth century it was a revolutionary idea. The most senior Army officers, led by Henry Ireton, Cromwell's son-in-law, were totally against it. Ireton said that only those 'with a permanent fixed interest in the kingdom' – land and property owners – should be allowed to take part in government. The Levellers and many other soldiers also wanted to abolish the monarchy, and stop Cromwell and other senior officers from negotiating with the King. Cromwell thought this was going too far. Cromwell's true opinion of the Levellers was expressed to the Council of State in 1649. He was not, as in 1647, trying to keep the peace in the Army, but attacking them as dangerous revolutionaries.

John Lilburne. The most outspoken of the Levellers, and their most influential man of ideas.

> I tell you Sir, you have no other way to deal with these men but to break them or they will break you; yea, and bring all the guilt of the blood and treasure shed and spent in the kingdom upon your heads and shoulders ... so render you to all rational men in the world as the most contemptible generation of silly, low-spirited men in the earth to be broken and raised by such a despicable, contemptible generation of men as they are ... I tell you again, you are necessitated to break them.

On two occasions, once in November 1647 and again in April 1649, Cromwell was forced to take tough action against Leveller mutinies in the Army. Not only were their ideas too revolutionary for him, but the Levellers were also a threat to military discipline, with their questioning attitudes and skill at political organisation. Cromwell's resistance to them reassured the property-owning classes and increased their confidence in him. As a landowner from a family of landowners, it would have been surprising if he had thought otherwise.

Henry Ireton by Robert Walker. An outstanding administrator and politician, he married Cromwell's daughter Bridget.

1 Make a list of reasons for breaking the Levellers from the point of view of Henry Ireton.

2 Discuss some of the reasons for the spread of Leveller ideas during the years of the English Civil War.

Stage 3   1649–51, the Crowning Mercy

Cromwell's personal influence was increased by the military success of 1648 and by his contribution to the removal of the King, but he was not yet the leader of the country. He was certainly recognised as the champion of the Independents, but he shared political decision-making with the other 40 members of the Council of State, who were themselves responsible to Parliament.

His next contribution to the new government was to complete the elimination of all remaining Royalist support. This took place in Ireland in 1649 and in Scotland and England in 1650–51. In Ireland, Cromwell carried out a brilliant campaign with great harshness. To him, the Irish Catholic Royalists were 'barbarous wretches'. He was carrying out the judgement of God on them. In 1650, by now Commander-in-Chief or 'Lord-General' because Fairfax had resigned, he invaded Scotland. The Scots were supporting the restoration of Charles' son as King Charles II. Cromwell's victory at Dunbar on 3 September was followed on the same date a year later by what he called 'The Crowning Mercy', the final destruction of the Scots and English Royalists at Worcester.

In stage 3 even greater military success as Lord-General of the Army raised his status to undisputed 'Chief of Men', as the poet Milton described him.

■ If the Royalists had tried Cromwell, what would have been some of the charges against him?

Stage 4   'What is the Lord adoing?', 1651–3

On 2 October 1651, Cromwell wrote to a friend in Boston, Massachusetts:

> How shall we behave ourselves after such mercies? What is the Lord adoing? What prophecies are now fulfilling? Who is a God like ours? To know his will, to do his will are both of him.

He certainly felt that he had been called by God to play a leading part in the settlement of the country. He also felt very strongly that no revolutionary social and political changes should be introduced, as he had shown in his opposition to the Levellers. He was, we must remember, a country landowner whose family fortunes had always depended on security of property. Property owners met in Parliament. He himself was an MP who respected its traditions. The Army's victories had been gained in the name of Parliamentary authority. Should not Parliament now be the supreme power?

Parliament at this time meant the 'Rump', or remainder, of the MPs first elected in the summer of 1640. There were many vacancies caused by death or resignation, and many soldiers felt that the Army was more representative of the people than the Rump. They wanted to dissolve the Rump by force, and supervise the election of a new Parliament. Cromwell, an MP himself and a great respecter of Parliament, argued for a peaceful, voluntary dissolution. But the Rump refused, and in the end Cromwell lost patience. On 20 April 1653, he made a speech at first thanking the Parliament for their efforts in the war, but then proceeded to attack them for corruption, drunkenness and blasphemy. His language was violent, his anger extreme, his behaviour shocking to the MPs. He shouted.

> Perhaps you think this is not parliamentary language. I confess it is not, neither are you to expect any such from me.... It is not fit you should sit as a Parliament any longer. You have sat long enough unless you had done more good.

Then he called in soldiers to clear out the MPs. The symbol of Parliamentary authority, the mace, he described as a 'bauble'. 'Take it away,' he ordered.

Thomas Harrison, soldier, and leader of the religious 'radicals'; too extreme for Cromwell.

A Dutch print of Cromwell dissolving the Rump Parliament.

What now? Major-General Thomas Harrison had an answer which Cromwell liked greatly: an assembly of 'saints', a carefully selected gathering of those men 'fearing God and of approved fidelity and honesty'. It was agreed and 140 members were elected. This *was* a 'revolutionary' idea. Cromwell approved because it seemed to be God's answer to their problems – a 'godly' Parliament. He spoke to the new assembly as follows:

> Truly you are called by God to rule with him and for him.... This may be the door to *usher* [welcome] in the things that God has promised, which have been prophesied of, which he has set the hearts of his people to wait for and expect.... You are at the edge of the promises and prophecies.

It was what he had fought for, but it failed him. The assembly, instead of agreeing on a programme to fulfil God's promises, behaved like a normal Parliament. At first the radicals were in control, suggesting changes in the law and in the taxation system. This worried the more conservative members who feared that 'property' was under attack again. It also seriously worried Major-General John Lambert and several other senior Army officers who were also big landowners. Lambert and his supporters in the assembly planned an early morning meeting for 12 December 1653, and, before the radicals could get there, voted to dissolve the assembly and give all power to Oliver Cromwell as Lord Protector. The document authorising this was called the Instrument of Government. Cromwell believed that John Lambert and his supporters were God's messengers, giving him the supreme authority that he had so far been reluctant to accept. On 16 December 1653, he was installed as Lord Protector in Westminster Abbey. In stage 4 we see Cromwell, the successful Lord-General accepting personal power when Parliament fails to perform satisfactorily.

John Lambert by Robert Walker. A brilliant soldier, and a sharp politician. Virtually Cromwell's deputy 1653–7.

1 Write a short newspaper article describing Cromwell dissolving the Rump on 20 April 1653. Choose a snappy headline.

2 What similarities and differences are there between the ways Oliver and Thomas Cromwell rose to power?

The House of Commons in 1651, as shown on the Seal of the Commonwealth.

39

The Cromwell family in power

This section will describe the new ruling family's lifestyle, and show how the marriages of Cromwell's daughters helped to strengthen the family's influence. It will also introduce you to his two surviving sons.

Oliver Cromwell had been well rewarded for his military and political services even before he became Lord Protector. In 1646 he had been given several estates previously belonging to defeated Royalists, worth about £2,500 per year in income. After the battle of Worcester, the triumphant Lord-General was rewarded with more estates, this time worth £4,000 per year. Once installed as Lord Protector, he was given the use of several former royal palaces in and around London. From April 1654, his main London residence was Whitehall Palace and his country retreat was Hampton Court Palace, where he used to go often from Friday to Monday. Not all his family were thrilled about Whitehall: Edmund Ludlow wrote that

Elizabeth, Oliver's wife, as Protectoress.

> His wife seemed at first unwilling to remove thither, though afterwards she became better satisfied with her grandeur; but his mother, who by reason of her great age was not so easily flattered with these temptations, very much mistrusted the issue of affairs.

Furniture and works of art, enjoyed previously by Charles I and worth about £35,000, were made available to Cromwell. The reception rooms of the palaces were redecorated with great splendour. This was not for Cromwell's personal, self-indulgent delight, but because it was felt that the new rulers must look like rulers, and receive their important visitors with style and dignity.

In private, the Cromwells lived much more simply than Charles I's family. The Venetian Ambassador commented on their 'unpretending manner of life' which he said was 'so different from the former fashion of the kingdom'. Henry Fletcher, generally a reliable writer, wrote (in 1660) about Cromwell's taste in food

A sixteenth-century print of Hampton Court Palace. (Only part of it is shown.)

French delicacies fashionable food and manners

> Spare, not curious.... At his private table very rarely, or never, were our French *quelque choses* suffered by him, or any such *modern gustos*.

According to an unkind Royalist writer, Elizabeth Cromwell always used cheap cuts of meat, liked marrow pudding for breakfast and kept cows in St

James' Park. The Protector allowed himself one very personal luxury: a special *close-stool* (portable toilet), decorated with red velvet, was brought over from Greenwich Palace for him!

For relaxation outdoors, Oliver would go hunting and hawking, traditional recreations of a country gentleman. Indoors, music was his great love. He had an organ transferred from Oxford to Hampton Court, and had another one in London. He employed eight musicians and two boys in training on his household staff. He loved English songs and madrigals, but disapproved of music in church. The first English operas were produced during his reign as Protector, public evidence of Cromwell's private love of music.

Cromwell was very much a family man: he had six sisters for whom he continued to feel responsible, especially the unmarried Jane and the widowed Catherine. He had five sons and four daughters. His eldest son Robert had died in 1637, aged 16, his second, Oliver, died of disease on active service during the war aged 21; Richard and Henry we shall meet again. A baby boy James died in 1632. His four daughters were all alive in the 1650s, and their marriages were important events naturally for the girls themselves, but also for extending Cromwell's family connections with other landowning families. Bridget, born in 1624, had first married Henry Ireton, one of Cromwell's leading colleagues and, after his death in 1651, her second husband was another senior Army officer, Charles Fleetwood. Elizabeth, born in 1629, was married in 1646 to John Claypole whose family were landowners near Ely.

John Claypole. Husband of Elizabeth Cromwell, Oliver's favourite daughter.

Bridget Cromwell. More serious-minded than her three younger sisters, she was married to two of her father's leading supporters.

Charles Fleetwood, second husband of Bridget Cromwell. Cromwell once referred to him as a 'milksop'.

Once Cromwell became Protector, the marriages of his remaining daughters Mary, born in 1637, and Frances, born in 1638 became important political as well as family events. On 11 November 1657, Frances married Robert Rich, a grandson of the Earl of Warwick, one of the nobles who supported Parliament against Charles I. (Some evidence exists to suggest that three years previously, a marriage between her and the exiled Charles II was being discussed!) Her wedding was celebrated in great style: 48 violins, 50 trumpets, and dancing (*mixed* dancing, shocking to some) till 5 a.m. According to one (probable) eye-witness, Oliver Cromwell really let his hair down.

hot milk curdled with sherry

wig

The Protector threw about *sack posset* among all the ladies to soil their rich clothes, which they took as a favour, and also wet sweetmeats and dawbed all the stools, where they were to sit with wet sweetmeats: and pull'd off Rich his *perucque*, and would have thrown it into the fire, but did not, yet he sat upon it.

On 19 November 1657, Cromwell's daughter Mary married Thomas Belasyse, Lord Fauconberg, whose family had large estates in Durham, Lancashire and Yorkshire. Most of his family were Royalists. Cromwell hoped that this marriage would help to make peace with former enemies. This marriage lasted 43 years, but Frances was a widow after three months.

Mary Cromwell. The most like her father of all the children, according to several historians.

Thomas Belasyse, Lord Fauconberg. Mary Cromwell's Royalist husband.

Cromwell's sons also had their part to play as members of the new ruling family. Richard, born in 1626, was a worry to his father. He seemed to take life too easily and not do enough serious reading and thinking. When he married Dorothy Mayor in 1646, his father relied on 'Doll' to keep Richard sensibly occupied. He wrote to her:

> As for the pleasures of this life, and outward business, *let that be upon the bye* [don't attach any importance to it]. Be above all these things, by faith in Christ, and then you shall have the true use and comfort of them, and not otherwise.

Most people thought that Richard was a great disappointment, lacking his father's 'high spirit and deep knowledge'. From 1655, he was given a job in the government. As the eldest surviving son, he might have to follow his father as Protector. We shall continue his story in the next chapter.

Richard Cromwell. Third son of Oliver, and the least suited of all his children for a career in public life.

Henry Cromwell, born in 1628, was a brighter and more energetic young man. At 16 he joined the New Model Army. At 21 he was a Colonel, at 25 an MP and in 1655 became Lord-Lieutenant (Governor) of Ireland. Being Oliver's son helped his career, but intelligence, hard work and strength of character played an equal part. Having got rid of a bossy advisor who treated him 'as a tutor guardian to a minor', Henry did his best to keep the peace between the various political, religious and military groups. He refused to accept an income drawn from estates in Ireland because he did not want to profit personally from a poor country for which he was responsible. His father sent him lots of advice, but the distance between Ireland and England meant that Henry was his own boss most of the time.

1 Make a family tree of Oliver Cromwell's children (his wife was Elizabeth Bourchier, remember). Give their dates of birth and death.

2 Write a short description of 'An evening with the Cromwells'.

3 Make up a conversation between Oliver Cromwell and his 88-year-old mother, in which he tries to persuade her that living in a palace and marrying his daughters to important people is politically necessary.

Henry Cromwell. Fourth son of Oliver, and an able administrator in Ireland.

43

'Let God be Judge between you and me!'

From 1653–8, Oliver Cromwell and his family lived in palaces, were addressed as 'Their Highnesses', and received important foreign visitors with great ceremony. Oliver's success, as we have seen, had been rewarded by grants of land. His daughters had made good marriages, and if one of his sons was rather ordinary, the other was winning respect as the ruler of Ireland. This was the high point of the fortunes of the family.

The Power of The Protector

How much power did Oliver Cromwell have as Lord Protector of Britain? Was he a military dictator with supreme power? The box below summarises the checks on his personal power.

Oliver Cromwell by Samuel Cooper, 1656.

Check No. 1: **Parliament.** The traditional law-making authority; could veto (stop) any decision of the Lord Protector and control money supply for government, including the Army; some members, known as 'republicans', opposed the idea of a personal Head of State; suspicious of the Army's power and influence.

Check No. 2: **The Army.** The brute strength in the land; a very efficient fighting force; many senior officers were 'republicans' and would oppose too much power being given to Cromwell; suspicious of Parliament since 1647; generally loyal to Cromwell.

Check No. 3: **The Council of State.** An advisory group for the Protector; dominated by Cromwell's character and reputation; some members were senior Army officers, some MPs, others clever public servants like John Thurloe.

Check No. 4: **Oliver Cromwell himself.** Cromwell did not want supreme personal power; believed deeply in Parliamentary government; loyal to Army, but recognised its power as 'non traditional'; saw himself as a peacemaker, a balancer of opposing forces to achieve a settlement.

John Thurloe. A key man in Cromwell's government, and an important historian of the period.

A brief description of some of the events of 1653–8 will show how difficult it was for Cromwell to achieve a peaceful settlement. The first Parliament of the Protectorate met on 3 September 1654 (that date again!). Cromwell had high hopes that there would be 'a sweet gracious and holy understanding of one another and your business'. The 'republicans' in the Parliament objected to the king-like power of Cromwell, the others demanded control over the Army. Cromwell dissolved the Parliament on 22 January 1655. In April 1655, a Royalist revolt in Wiltshire was defeated. Alarmed by the possibility of further unrest, Cromwell authorised the dividing up of the country into districts controlled by Major-Generals: this was a direct use of military force to make his government secure. It was expensive, so Cromwell had to call another Parliament to grant the money to pay for the system. In January 1657 the new Parliament refused to grant the money. Cromwell had to agree to abandon the Major-Generals. Then Parliament offered to make him King.

John Desborough. Married Cromwell's sister Anne. One of the controlling Major-Generals in 1655. 'The Grim Giant' according to a Royalist enemy.

King Oliver?

Should he take the title? What a magnificent achievement to make yourself the king, with the chance of establishing your family as the Royal Family. If he did become king, with a new House of Lords and a traditional House of Commons, would it not be an admirable, traditional, widely acceptable settlement?

After much hesitation he refused the Crown, mainly because his senior Army colleagues would have resigned if he had not.

So he agreed to carry on as Lord Protector, with a new House of Lords, and with the right to name his successor. On 4 February 1658, he dissolved his last uncooperative Parliament with the words 'Let God be Judge between you and me.' It is clear from his letters and speeches that he did not seek power for personal glory. He accepted the Protectorship, and he accepted those limitations on it that would make it acceptable to as many people as possible. He deeply respected Parliament, but his Parliament mistrusted his Army. Without the Army he could not control the country, and he felt loyalty and gratitude to the Army for the years of victory. Armies and Parliaments apart, the source of his personal strength was a belief in himself as God's instrument. This gave him the mental stamina to face the difficulties, to balance the opposing forces and the courage to take a hard decision when necessary.

1 To be King? Make two lists for Cromwell, one of reasons for, and another of reasons against.

2 Write a letter from an old soldier of Cromwell's, pleading with him not to accept the Crown.

Oliver Cromwell looking king-like on the Protectoral money. No evidence proves it was ever actually used.

'My design is to make what haste I can to be gone'

Oliver's favourite daughter was Elizabeth, married to John Claypole. During the Protectorate she, her husband and four children lived with Oliver at Hampton Court and Whitehall. She was less serious-minded than other Cromwells, an attractive, fun-loving girl whose father sometimes worried about her love of frivolous things and her wilful nature. He could refuse her nothing, and she often successfully pleaded for mercy to be shown to some poor Royalist prisoner. This extract from a poem by Andrew Marvell, who knew them both well, expresses the joy and closeness of their relationship.

> With her each day the pleasing hours he shares,
> And at her *aspect* [expression] calms his growing cares,
> Or with a *grandsire's* [grandfather's] joy her children sees
> Hanging about her neck or at his knees.

Sadly, by the summer of 1658, she was desperately ill, probably with cancer. In July, Oliver virtually gave up public business to be at her bedside. Marvell witnessed the grief-stricken father, trying to hide his sorrow as Elizabeth hid her pain as best she could.

> She, lest he grieve, hides what she can her pains,
> And he, to lessen hers, his sorrow *feigns* [pretends].

She died on 6 August aged 29. Oliver never fully recovered from his grief.

> It is one thing to have the greatest bough lopt off, but when the axe is laid to the root, then there is no hope remaining such was our real fear.

Those telling words were written by Richard Cromwell, who realised that his beloved sister's death might destroy his father. Oliver was too ill with grief to attend the funeral. On 17 August, George Fox, a leading Quaker who enjoyed many a tough argument with Cromwell over religion, saw him at Hampton Court.

> And I saw and felt a *waft* [wave] of death go forth against him that he looked like a dead man.

Elizabeth Claypole, by John Michael Wright, 1658. She is dressed as Minerva, daughter of Jupiter – a flattering reference to Cromwell. The clouded sky and shipwreck are sad references to her and her father's deaths.

Later that night, Cromwell fell ill. It seems to have been a serious kidney infection leading to blood poisoning. He fought the illness hard, drawing comfort from prayer and bible readings. They took him back to Whitehall Palace, where he died on 3 September 1658, the anniversary of two of his greatest battles.

> My work is done but God will be with his people. Thou hast made me, though very unworthy, a mean instrument to do them some good, and Thee service; and many of them have set too high a value upon me, though others wish and would be glad of my death; Lord, however Thou do dispose of me, continue and do good for them.

Oliver Cromwell lying in State after death. If this is accurate, he was given all the symbols of royalty.

Who would succeed him? He had the right to name the person. Nothing existed in writing, but during his last illness he had nodded 'Yes' to the name of his elder son Richard. Many would have chosen the more experienced and energetic Henry. Oliver probably had two reasons for naming Richard:

1. He was the elder son.

2. Henry had more enemies and rivals.

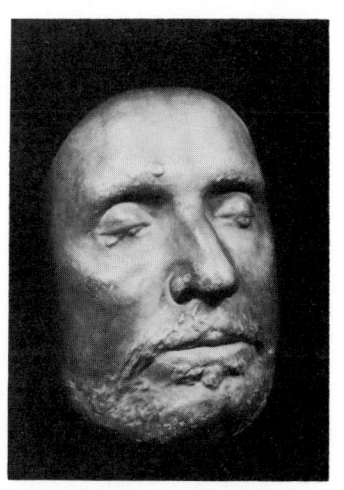

Death mask of Cromwell.

Richard Cromwell.

Richard Cromwell became the Lord Protector, but he lacked his father's personal strength and political influence. Rival groups within the Army quarrelled and another Parliament merely added to the confusion. Richard was forced to resign by a group of generals, and, in the end, General Monck took charge and supervised the calling of Parliament which voted to bring back the monarchy. King Charles II returned in May 1660.

What happened to the Cromwells? Under Oliver, the family had enjoyed power, prestige and riches. Oliver Cromwell's reputation for strong government was very good in foreign countries. Now that the son of the king whom Cromwell had destroyed was himself the monarch, would not a terrible revenge be taken? Oliver's body was certainly punished. The corpse was dragged through the streets of London and the head hacked off and stuck on a pole outside Westminster Hall. It was not taken down until 1684. No living members of the family suffered any physical hurt. In 1660, Elizabeth, Oliver's wife, was accused of hiding in a fruiterer's warehouse some jewels and pictures that had belonged to the royal family. This led her to present a petition to Charles II, denying the charge and asking to be allowed to retire quietly. There was no evidence against her. She was allowed to go free and live in Northamptonshire with the Claypoles, her dead daughter Elizabeth's husband's family. She died there in 1665.

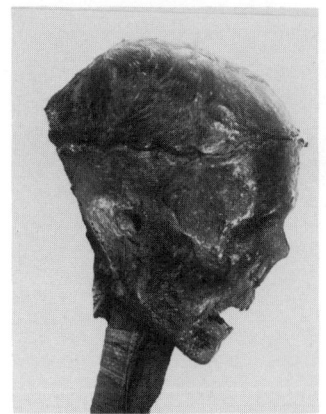

The skeletal head of Oliver Cromwell, now buried near the Chapel of Sidney Sussex College, Cambridge.

'The humble petition of Elizabeth Cromwell, Widow' (An extract)

She is deeply *sensible* [aware] of those unjust *imputations* [accusations] whereby she is charged of detaining jewels and other goods belonging to your Majesty; which, besides the disrepute of it, hath exposed her to many violences and losses under pretence of searching for such goods, to the undoing of her in her estate and rendering her *abode* [residence] in any place unsafe; – She being willing to depose upon oath that she neither hath nor knows of any such jewels or goods. . . . She hath never intermeddled in any of those public transactions which have been *prejudicial* [harmful] to your Majesty's royal father or yourself, and is ready to yield an humble and faithful obedience to your Majesty in your Government.

Richard Cromwell left the country in 1660, leaving his wife and children behind in Hampshire. He lived in Paris for a time, where he spent much time reading and drawing landscapes, and he may also have visited Italy and Spain. He lived nervously, under assumed names, worried about debts, royalist assassins bent on revenge, and enemies of King Charles II trying to involve him in plots. He was allowed to return to England in 1680. He lived at Cheshunt, in Hertfordshire, calling himself John Clarke. His wife Dorothy had died five years earlier. He lived until 1712. In a letter to his daughter Anne, written on 18 December 1690, he said

> I have been alone thirty years *banished* [forced to live abroad] and under silence; and my strength and safety is to be retired, quiet and silent. We are foolish in taking our cause out of the hand of God.

Henry Cromwell and his sisters, Bridget, Mary and Frances were not considered dangerous by Charles II, and did not suffer punishment. Henry was allowed to keep most of his estates and died at Spinney Abbey, Cambridgeshire in 1674. Bridget died in 1662. Mary lived until 1713. Her husband Lord Fauconberg became a rich and successful man, held important government jobs and was made an Earl. Mary was a great lady at Court, famous for her sharp wit, and robust pride in her father's achievements. Because of her important position she was able to make life a little easier for her relations. She was described in later life as 'a great and curious piece of antiquity'. Her sister Frances died in 1721, aged 84. She survived her second husband by 51 years, spending much of her time with her sister Mary.

King Charles II by John Michael Wright.

Mary and Frances were proud of their father, but some of Oliver's Royalist cousins changed their name back from Cromwell to Williams.

What can we say about the rise and fall of the Cromwell family in the days of Oliver and his children? Their rise was the achievement of Oliver. His political and military skills, his force of character, his inner strength and physical stamina, his search for balance, harmony and co-operation made him the driving force and stabilising influence of the Revolution. Rewards of land strengthened his family's position in the country's power structure. Oliver's care over his children's marriages paid off after his death. Despite Richard's debts and Henry's loss of some land, Oliver's daughters-in-law and daughters passed on to their descendants the economic strength of the landowning class. Political power, as enjoyed by Thomas Cromwell in the sixteenth century and Oliver in the seventeenth century would never return.

1 Make two lists: one headed 'Oliver Cromwell's successes' the other 'Oliver Cromwell's failures'.
Compare lists and discuss the differences.

2 An 'obituary' is a newspaper article about someone who has died. Write 150 words summing up Cromwell's life and achievements.

3 Make up a conversation between Charles II and Mary Fauconberg about Oliver Cromwell. You may need to find out a little about Charles II's character first.

Find out more for yourself

1. Find out more about your own family's identity today. What does your surname mean? What relics of your ancestors do you have? What motto or arms would you devise for your family? What items would you wish to hand on to your descendants to remind them of you? Make some comparisons between the way of life of your family today and a family of the early seventeenth century – for example, family size.

2. Find out more about your ancestors. Draw up your family tree as far as you can go. Make a catalogue of the evidence you use to build your diagram – documents, pictures, inscriptions on gravestones, etc.

3. Find out more about objects or sites that will help you to understand the Cromwell family, or the times they lived in. Look in local museums for the sort of furniture they might have had – some very grand, but also sturdy domestic cupboards, tables, pots and pans. Thomas would have spent much time at Henry VIII's royal palaces, such as Hampton Court. Did Oliver Cromwell pass by your area? He lived in Huntingdon, St Ives and Ely, went to college in Cambridge and campaigned throughout England, Ireland, Scotland and Wales (see the guide to battlefields, below).

4. Here are some books to help you find out more about subjects mentioned in this book. Those marked * are reference books.

Published by Longman:

A Prisoner's Life in the Tower, D Birt

The Great Cardinal, D Birt and I Carstairs

King and Pope, D Birt and I Carstairs

Tudor London, D Birt and I Carstairs

The Civil War, D Birt and J Nichol

Cromwell, D Birt and J Nichol

*J Brooke-Little, *An Heraldic Alphabet*, Macdonald and Jane's, 1973

*B Cottle, *The Penguin Dictionary of Surnames*, Allen Lane, 1978, (2nd edn.)

*Ottfried Neubecker, *A Guide to Heraldry*, Cassell, 1979

*P H Reaney, *A Dictionary of British Surnames*, Routledge and Kegan Paul, 1976, (2nd edn.)

*D K Smurthwaite, *Ordnance Survey guide to the battlefields of Britain*, Webb and Bower, Ordnance Survey

Index

arms, coats of 5
Austin Friars 17, 18, 22, 23

babies, survival of 11
Beard, Dr Thomas 27

Charles I 27, 28, 34, 35
Charles II 48, 49
Claypole, John 41
Cranmer, Archbishop 8, 21
Council of State 36, 37, 44
Cromwell, Bridget 41
Cromwell, Elizabeth (sister of Thomas) 1
Cromwell, Elizabeth (wife of Thomas) 9, 10, 11
Cromwell, Elizabeth (née Bourchier; wife of Oliver) 28, 40, 48
Cromwell, Elizabeth (mother of Oliver) 27, 40
Cromwell, Elizabeth (daughter of Oliver) 41, 46
Cromwell, Grace and Anne 11
Cromwell, Gregory 5, 9, 10, 16, 18, 19, 23
Cromwell, Sir Henry (The Golden Knight) 26
Cromwell, Henry (son of Oliver) 26
Cromwell, Katherine 11, 24
Cromwell, Mary 42, 49
Cromwell, Sir Oliver (uncle of Oliver) 26
Cromwell, Oliver 27–49
Cromwell, Richard (son of Oliver) 43, 47, 48, 49
Cromwell, Robert 27
Cromwell, Thomas 8–23
Cromwell, Walter 8, 10, 11, 18, 24

Digby, Lord 30
Dunbar 37

Edgehill 31

Fairfax, Sir Thomas 33, 35
Family Tree 6, 7, 24
Fauconberg, Lord (Thomas Belasyse) 42
Fleetwood, Charles 41
Fox, George 46
Foxe, John 8

Hampton Court Palace 40
Hampden, John 30, 31
Harrison, Major-General Thomas 39
Henry VIII 12, 20, 21, 22, 23, 25
Hinchingbrooke House 26, 27
Holles, Denzil 34
Huntingdon 28

Ireton, Henry 36, 41

Lambert, Major-General John 39
Levellers 36
Lilburne, John 30, 36

Major-Generals 45
Manchester, Earl of 31, 33
marriage 9, 10, 11, 19, 21

Marston Moor 32
Mary, Princess 10, 19, 21

Naseby 33
New Model Army 31, 33
Norfolk, Duke of 20

Parliaments 30, 38, 39, 45, 48
Pilgrimage of Grace 16

Rainsborough, Col. Thomas 36
Rich, Robert 42

St John, Mrs 29
St John, Oliver 30
Self-Denying Ordinance 35
Seymour, Elizabeth 19
Seymour, Jane 19
Sidney Sussex College, Cambridge 28
Smyth, Walter and Thomas, alias Cromwell 8, 9
Spinney Abbey 49
surnames 3, 4, 25

Walton, Valentine 32
Wellyfed family 11, 18
Whitehall Palace 40
widows 9, 19
Williams, Richard, alias Cromwell 16, 23, 24
Wolsey, Cardinal Thomas 12, 14, 16, 23
Worcester 37
Wykys, Elizabeth 9, 10, 11

Acknowledgements

The authors would particularly like to thank the following for their help: Douglas Clinton, Diana Freke, Mark Eller, Anne Cooper and Brenda Cusworth.

The authors and publishers are grateful to the following for permission to reproduce material:

Ashmolean Museum, Oxford, page 40; BBC Hulton Picture Library, pages 38 and 48; British Library, page 39; British Museum, page 5; Trustees of the Chatsworth Settlement, Devonshire Collection/Courtauld Institute of Art, page 8; Chequers Trust/Courtauld Institute of Art, pages 27, 41, 42, 43 and 48; Cromwell Museum, Huntingdon, pages 26, 27 and 32; Mary Evans Picture Library, page 36; John Freeman and Co., page 47; Museum of London, page 29; National Army Museum, page 31; National Gallery, page 9; National Portrait Gallery, pages 7, 10, 12, 15, 19, 21, 22, 23, 29, 30, 32, 33, 34, 35, 36, 38, 41, 42, 43, 44, 45, 46, 47 and 49; Marquess of Tavistock and the Trustees of the Bedford Estate, page 19; Victoria and Albert Museum, pages 16 and 17; Victoria and Albert Museum/private collection, page 28.

The pictures on pages 20 and 25 are reproduced by gracious permission of Her Majesty the Queen.

Every attempt has been made to contact copyright holders, but we apologise if any have been overlooked.

A World of Change

This book is part of a series entitled *A World of Change*, intended for the 11–14 age group. The aim of the whole series is to combine a firm framework of historical fact with a 'skill-based' approach. The factual content provides continuity, and the opportunity to study causation and development. It is balanced by the two other vital ingredients for lively study of history: opportunity for 'empathy', which enables children to make an imaginative leap into the past; and study of a variety of original sources, both written and visual.

The series comprises a core textbook which studies a number of themes important in the Early Modern Age, approximately 1450–1700; a number of linked topic books; and a teacher's book for the whole series (which includes copyright-free worksheets).

The core book is primarily concerned with the British Isles, but within the context of what was happening in the rest of the world, known and unknown. The well-known political, religious and economic themes are considered. So too are the lives of ordinary men, women and children, and the way in which both change and continuity affected them. The book does not set out to be a full chronological survey, but it is hoped that it is sufficiently flexible to be used in that way if desired.

The core textbook is complete in itself, but has also been designed to provide a number of stepping-off points for 'patch studies'. Opportunities for this kind of work are provided by the eight *World of Change* topic books which are clearly linked to the themes in the main book. However, the topic books are also designed so that they can be used on their own if desired. All the topic books are listed on the back cover.

For the teacher

The *Teacher's Book* for the World of Change series contains additional suggestions for reading and follow-up activities.

Suggestions for background reading on the two main characters include:

For Thomas:

Life and Letters of Thomas Cromwell, R B Merriman, 2 vols, Thomas' will (12 July 1529) is well worth further study, and is published as an Appendix to Chapter III.

An inventory of his property at Austin Friars (26 June 1527) is published in

Letters and Papers, foreign and domestic, of the reign of Henry VIII, ed., Brewer, Gairdner and Brodie, 18 vols, (1862–1902) vol. iv, 3197. These are available at Public Record Offices.

For Oliver:

W C Abbott (ed.), *Writings and Speeches of Oliver Cromwell* (4 vols), Cambridge (Mass.), 1937–47

C H Firth, *Cromwell's Army*, Methuen, 1962

Antonia Fraser, *Cromwell, our Chief of Men*, Methuen, 1985 (originally Weidenfeld 1973)

Christopher Hill, *God's Englishman*, Pelican, 1985 (and earlier printings)

P Young and R Holmes, *The English Civil War – A Military History of the Three Civil Wars, 1642–51*, Eyre Methuen, 1974

© John Cooper and Susan Morris 1987

All rights reserved. No part of this publication may be reproduced, stored in a retrieval system or transmitted in any form or by any means, electronic, mechanical, photocopying, recording or otherwise, without the prior written consent of the copyright holders. Applications for such permission should be addressed to the publishers: Stanley Thornes (Publishers) Ltd, Old Station Drive, Leckhampton, CHELTENHAM GL53 0DN, England.

First published in 1987 by:
Stanley Thornes (Publishers) Ltd
Old Station Drive
Leckhampton
CHELTENHAM GL53 0DN
England

Typeset by Tech-Set, Gateshead, Tyne & Wear
Printed and bound in Great Britain by
Ebenezer Baylis and Son Ltd, Worcester

British Library Cataloguing in Publication Data

Cooper, John
   The Cromwell family. — (A World of change).
   1. Great Britain — History — Tudors,
   1485–1603 2. Great Britain — History —
   Stuarts, 1603–1714
   I. Title   II. Morris, Susan   III. Series
   942.05   DA315

ISBN 0-85950-546-4